STAND FIRM

From the Darkness of Pornography and Sexual Sin
into the Light of God's Grace

by Lynn Fredrick

"Lynn Fredrick is one of those deeply dedicated Christian men who has worked an exemplary program. We need more testimonies like this one so as to encourage all of us."

Dr. Mark Laaser, M.Div., Ph.D.
Founder of Faithful and True, www.faithfulandtrue.com

"I have known Lynn Fredrick for almost ten years, and serve as pastor of the church he writes about in *Stand Firm*. I have been a part of his progress from suspect church member to church team leader to elder. In this book, Lynn chronicles the foundation of that process—a journey that few people dare to attempt: a journey to the center of one's self. There Lynn has looked evil in the eye with the weapons of God's grace, and has overcome. *Stand Firm* is a candid and practical resource for anyone that is fighting an addiction, or for any sinner who needs help in overcoming themselves."

Donn Schroeder
Senior Pastor, First Church of Christ, Ladysmith, WI

"With much rigorous honesty, transparency, and vulnerability, Lynn Fredrick makes his life an open book in conversationally walking us through his journey into—and out of—sexual addiction. This rich and helpful book will offer great hope to others facing similar struggles."

Mark Halvorsen
Talk Show Host, WWIB Christian Radio,
Co-founder of Teamwork Africa

"Lynn's story is real, his struggle is real, and his approach to recovery is real. The strategies, scriptural basis, and positive approach are real. Stand Firm is a road map to recovery and a practical, Bible-based, step-by-step, honest approach. This is a book of hope."

Mark Bergen
Professional Counselor, State of Wisconsin

"*Stand Firm* is a brutally honest confession of a wonderful man whose 'life' was destroyed by his slavery to sexual addiction. This is a heart-wrenching yet hope-filled recollection of Lynn's recovery journey, from those inaudible voices telling him to 'pull the trigger' to the Promised Land of living twenty-four years without secrets and shame. Restored to new life by the light of God's grace is more than a cliché for this author; it is his reality, and he offers us that same opportunity. Thank you for your courage and compassion, Lynn Fredrick."

Deacon Craig Voldberg
Parish Life Coordinator for the Rusk County Catholic Community in the Diocese of Superior, WI

"In recent years, I've read several books about the issue of pornography and its negative impact on our culture. Lynn Fredrick, in *Stand Firm*, not only chronicles his personal journey to freedom, but he also offers a path to hope for anyone in bondage. This book is biblically sound, practical, and encouraging. I highly recommend it!"

Pastor Kurt W. Bubna
Author of *Epic Grace: Chronicles of a Recovering Idiot*

STAND FIRM: From the Darkness of Pornography and Sexual Sin into the Light of God's Grace

Copyright © 2017 by Lynn Fredrick
All rights reserved.

This book or any portion thereof may not be reproduced or used in any manner whatsoever without the express written permission of the publisher except for the use of brief quotations in a book review.

Printed in the United States of America
Published in association with Athanatos Publishing Group
ISBN-13: 978-1947844001

All Scripture quotations, unless otherwise indicated, are taken from the Holy Bible, New International Version®, NIV®. Copyright ©1973, 1978, 1984, 2011 by Biblica, Inc.™ Used by permission of Zondervan. All rights reserved worldwide. www.zondervan.com The "NIV" and "New International Version" are trademarks registered in the United States Patent and Trademark Office by Biblica, Inc.™

Editing: Blake Atwood with BA Writing Solutions LLC.

This book is dedicated to my Higher Power,
"who came to all mankind from heaven;
to shine on those living in darkness and in the shadow of death,
to guide our feet into the path of peace" (Luke 1:78b-79).

You have raised me from the death of addiction,
restored me to sanity,
and have brought me serenity and contentment.
I give this book and it's testimony to you for your glory.

I share this book with all you bring to read it
in the hope you will lead them as you have led me
from the darkness of shame
into the light of your awesome grace.

ACKNOWLEDGMENTS

A special acknowledgment to my wife Terry: you have lived and loved me through the recall of my past secret life and in the darkness stood by me and encouraged me through the countless hours of writing my story of God leading me on the journey from shame to grace. God has definitely gifted me with the most wonderful companion in this life's great adventure. I love you back.

Special thanks to my daughter, my church elders, Mark Bergen and Lynn Farley, for editorial comments, encouragement, and all your help in the early days of my manuscript, and to Blake Atwood for your gift in editing and your kind and gentle writing solutions.

To my church family: you have heard me speak on aspects of this book from the podium and in small group Bible study for many years. Thank you for cheering me on and encouraging me to bring this book to print.

Thank you Mark Laaser for your gentle shepherding, leading me to a greener pasture, and for teaching me to practice, practice, practice.

Thank you to all the people I have met over eleven years of attending weekly recovery groups and mostly only know by first name. You accepted me at the lowest point in my life and led me on the path to trust in the power greater than myself.

AN INVITATION TO THE READER
from Lynn Fredrick's wife, Terry

We live in a world of light and darkness, good and evil. We can choose to rise out of the darkness and look to God for his light that burns eternally. My husband, Lynn made that choice.

In my mind, he is like a modern-day Moses who went searching for the Promised Land. As he stood on the shore of his Red Sea, stained within and full of shame, he turned his will over to God. Then God took him by the hand and led him on a journey to the freedom that is found in God's love and grace on the other side.

Come, now is the time to learn what Lynn has to share about his awesome journey. Lynn's story speaks of his insights of love, the wisdom God has placed in his heart, the power of faith, and the beauty of God's truth and promises that are available when you trust in the power of God.

Don't be afraid. You are well-companioned on this journey. Travel on with faith, with courage in your heart.

Beyond the darkness, behold: God's light and grace!

— Terry L. Fredrick

CONTENTS

Dedication vii

Acknowledgments ix

An Invitation to the Reader xi

Introduction 1

Prologue: Trails End 3

1: Wandering in the Wilderness 5

2: Crossing Your Red Sea 17

3: The Great Adventure 33

4: Pursue 71

5: The Promised Land 85

The 12 Steps of Alcoholics Anonymous, Adapted .. 103

Endnotes 105

Credits and Sources of Help 107

About the Author 109

INTRODUCTION

As a recovering sex addict with more than twenty years of sobriety from pornography, I've spoken to a variety of groups about sexual addiction. I always parted those public education talks wishing for a do-over. I felt like I always left something out. I'd talk too much about statistics and the characteristics of sexual addiction. I feared that some things could have been better said by researchers and skilled therapists. Yet there remained within me the conviction that I have something beneficial to say and that God wanted to use my life. The result is this book: a practical, Bible-based guide to repentance and recovery from the habitual sin called addiction.

This guide will help anyone caught in the grip of addiction or any habit-driven desire, but it is directed toward Christians or anyone open to how the God of Judeo-Christian belief can and will restore broken lives. This book is intended to help anyone change their character defects and harmful behavior patterns to become a better person, one more reflective of the intent of our Creator. This book is not about statistics or theories about recovery. This is my story—my great adventure—of how God actually restored a fallen, broken, born-again, evangelical pastor and gave him a second chance.

This book details how my higher power, The Great Shepherd, led me away from my bondage to pornography, across my red sea, and through the wilderness to the promised land here on earth. I intend and hope that this book might be a road map to guide you on the same journey from shame to grace on which God has led me. The signs on this route point to God, his Word, his promises, his grace, and his divine power that he uses to do for us what we're unable to do for ourselves.

I praise God for raising me from the death of addiction and giving me a new life. In these pages, I believe you will come to know that he will do the same for anyone who chooses him as their higher power and follows him on this most great adventure.

As you'll read, my life now attests to how deeply I've been changed, but there's one particular characteristic that truly reveals God's impressive work on this recovering sex addict: when I share my story, I no longer feel like I've left something unsaid.

PROLOGUE: TRAILS END

I remember the voices.

They weren't audible, but they were so strong and powerful: "Just do it. It's one bullet."

This happened at the appropriately named Trails End, a primitive hunting shack located in a very remote wilderness. Accessible only by walking or ATV, Trails End was my escape. Sometimes I'd go there with my collection of paper prostitutes and spend a whole day lost in sexual fantasies. I'd drink alcohol too, a bad combination. I'd added a chemical depressant to the impending crash into despair that was sure to follow.

"Pull the trigger. No one will care or even miss you. If anything, they'll all be happy. You'll be doing yourself and the world a favor."

At the end of myself at Trails End, I barely heard the whisper: "No, don't do it."

I'm not confident as to how I survived that encounter with suicide, or any of the others, but I'm positive I don't want to be in that mental state ever again.

Years later, my addiction recovery sponsor asked me why I hadn't followed through with suicide. The only thing I could truthfully recall was that I'd thought of my children. He smiled and said it was the same thought that had saved him.

If you've had thoughts like these, please listen to the quiet voice that tells you, "No, don't do it." This book is about following that gentle, soft voice who will lead you to a better place.

I know that because I've been where you are and can't believe where I am now.

CHAPTER 1
WANDERING IN THE WILDERNESS

Years later, I almost lost my children, but in a vastly different way than I thought I would at Trails End. After returning home from fishing one day, I walked into our five-bedroom, monstrously quiet house. I discovered a note with my wife's handwriting: *Gone to my parents and I've taken the girls with me. Our son is at his friends for now. We may not come back. I want a divorce.*

Frantic and afraid, I called her parents' home to speak with her. Her father answered. His curt reply was only, "You have a very sick kind of love," then he hung up on me.

Ironically, it was a blessing in disguise. My fear of abandonment had come all too true and forced me to be honest about my problems for the first time. I called our marriage counselor, and for the first time ever I told someone else about my problem with pornography. But on this particular call, this man also became the first counselor to ever shut the door in my face for telling the truth.

This professional said he'd continue to work with my wife, but that I was too far gone to be helped. In that moment, I felt like I couldn't sink any lower. I was afraid that I would never be freed from the guilt and shame within, or from my obsession and compulsion with pornography. I felt *alone*, like there was no one else in the world as bad as me. I felt like no one else had whatever it was I had.

The counselor gave me a phone number for some secret group called the Augustine Fellowship and promptly hung up. In the silence that followed, my mind repeated his words: *too far gone?* At thirty-eight years old, I'd told the truth for the first time in order to seek help for my problem, and what was my reward? Rejection, abandonment, and loneliness.

With nowhere else to turn, I turned to the One who said he'd never forsake me. I sat down in a chair and let my Bible fall open, praying for some great revelation.

God, tell me what to do so all this will be better. I'll do it this time too. Honest.

My Bible just happened to fall open to Isaiah 66. I read that I had chosen my own way and had delighted in my abominations. When God called to me, I didn't listen. I did evil in his sight and chose what displeases him.

Ouch! There has to be a better message than this. Let's try that let-the-Bible-fall-open-thing one more time.

It fell to Isaiah 57:13: "When you cry out for help, let your collection of idols save you!"

I realized in an instant: *I'm an idolater.* My compulsion and obsession with pornography had become my god. The images of prostitutes were my Higher Power.

When the sun came up I dialed that mysterious number for the Augustine Fellowship. A gracious and helpful person assured me I was not alone and that there was help for me. Those words were an oasis to my parched, lonely soul. The volunteer worker also let me know of their new, national name: Sex and Love Addicts Anonymous (SLAA). I was given a phone number for a self-help group sixty-five miles away from my northern Wisconsin address, as well as a number for a treatment facility one hundred and forty miles away.

I was diagnosed at the treatment facility, but couldn't afford the cost of the treatment program. Consequently, I visited that SLAA group sixty-five miles away, but didn't feel comfortable around the other participants. I then visited a Sex Addicts Anonymous (SAA) group that was eighty miles away. I figured if I could drive such distances to get porn, I could sure drive those distances to get help for porn addiction. I felt much more comfortable with the people in that group.

For those currently struggling with finding a supportive group in which you feel comfortable, I've learned that the dynamics of every group are different. You may fit better in one than another, so you will serve yourself well if you keep looking for the right community in which to seek healing for your addiction.

I'll never forget how scared I was before my first meeting. Who are these people? What will they look like? Do they wear trench coats? Would someone of my successful upper-middle-class "greatness" fit in?

When I walked into that meeting, everyone looked normal. I would come to know these men and women as teachers, professors, college students, factory workers, pastors, and farmers—people from every walk of life. I had never been so accepted by any group of people in my life. They listened to my story of addiction without judgment or condemnation. They told their stories and assured me that if I worked the 12 Steps

I would find that my Higher Power would do for me what I could never do for myself.

In the coming years, from a secular college student half my age no less, I would learn more about the power of God than I ever had known. I had to learn how to trust someone besides myself, and began to trust this young man and then other people in our group. I began to understand that I had never fully trusted my Higher Power, the God of Abraham, as revealed to mankind in Christ Jesus.

I chose this Higher Power because I know of no other with so many historical accounts written by eyewitnesses who saw and experienced his life, death, and resurrection, which brought about the salvation that freed me from the power of my addiction. I needed a Higher Power who is alive and could raise someone from the dead, because that's what I was.

I'd been rejected by a counseling professional whom I'd paid, essentially, to not reject me.

My wife was close to abandoning me forever and taking my kids with her.

I was as alone as I'd ever been.

But through that group I learned that God had never rejected or abandoned me, and by no means had he ever left me alone, despite a long history of feeling completely abandoned.

How Did I Get Here?

Sexual abuse, physical abuse, and exposure to pornography all by the fourth grade set the patterns for my very confused belief system.

Around nine years old, I was sexually abused by a neighbor boy of around fifteen. I was betrayed into his hands by my middle brother, who knew that if he turned me over to this older boy, I wouldn't be tagging along behind him for a while. Within that same year and for the same reason, my brother approved of pornography given to me by a friend of his.

My brother had a lot of anger toward me. He once punched me in the arm until I thought it would fall off. On another occasion, he hunted me with a gun and threatened to kill me if he found me. I'd hide in the woods until I thought mom and dad were home from work. I'd try to tell them my side of the story but would end up defending myself against an older, stronger, and smarter brother. It doesn't take a college degree to know that when a third-grader goes up against a seventh-grader, the younger one will lose every time—like the time I almost lost an eye.

As farm kids, we fed the cows on a daily basis. On this particular day, I was feeding the cows silage, and my brother was upset that he had to feed the cows hay. As we met midway down the manger, a pitchfork full of hay on his shoulder, he threw the hay in my face. Only, he'd misjudged the distance between us. The pitchfork entered my head just below my lower eyelid, missing the pupil by an eighth of an inch. The tine had stopped at the edge of my brain.

I lived at a children's hospital for a while as doctors battled the infection intent on destroying my eye. The miraculous healing of my eye is another story. The point here is that my brother had convinced himself and my mother that I'd done something to cause the event and somehow deserved the result. To this day I battle the belief that I always need to defend myself. But now I know why and where it began.

I wanted my parents to know the truth of what had happened. I wanted my brother to be held responsible for his uncontrolled anger toward me. But my parents didn't want to take the time to know the truth. My brother got off scot-free and I suffered the consequences of his behavior.

My mom and dad were not mean people, just busy. In addition to the dairy farm, they both worked outside of the house, sometimes at several jobs. I was the youngest of three boys. My oldest brother was sixteen when I was born, and there were four years of school between the next brother and me. By the time I'd entered high school, I assumed my parents were burnt out on parenting. I was the only child left at home, and the workload was harder.

At sixteen, my parents confronted me between the house and the barn as I was on my way to complete my chores. "Are you going to take over the farm?" Looking back, it wasn't so much a question as a statement of fact. But at the time, I'd just finished helping a local carpenter build a new shed, and I'd really enjoyed the experience. I replied, "I think I'd like to become a carpenter some day." They simply said, "OK" and walked into the house. I didn't think anything of it.

But within a month, my parents had auctioned off the farm and moved to a different city! My dad had taken a job with a canning company. I guess he was tired of farm living, or me, or both. At least my parents offered me a choice: move with them and finish my last two years of high school in a new town twenty miles away, or stay in my current school, with my current friends, yet live with my brother, or on my own, or with my grandmother, and pay for my own way with whatever work I could find during the summers *and* during the school years.

For an almost-junior, the choice was obvious. I stayed.

Sometimes I felt pretty alone, especially in that small apartment just outside Minneapolis. My parents had put me in a hard place, and at a young age I had to make adult decisions most high school kids didn't have to deal with. I harbored anger against them for many years. I wished they would have waited to sell the farm until after I'd graduated. It was just two years.

Coincidentally, I'd been placed in the same position my father had when he was my age: alone and forced to make his own way in the world. I certainly learned how to take care of myself, but the best result of this trying time was twofold: my grandmother, Nora, got a second chance to be a better mother than ever before and to have a son she'd never had. We became very close. Grandma became the mother my natural mother never had the time to become. I wouldn't trade being with my grandmother for those two school years for anything in the world.

Even though my parents left me when I still needed help, they did leave me with something—a wound I didn't understand and one that would fester for many years: abandonment. Now that I'm older, I can see how everything about my hidden life after that point was a result of everything I'd endured. And that hidden life stole decades from me.

My Most Important Need

From youth I was drawn toward sexual stimulation. When things weren't going well with my parents, my brother, or life in general, my addiction brought some self-nurturing and comfort. I could always retreat to my bedroom in our large farmhouse and escape for a time into fantasy and sexual self-stimulation. That tendency would escalate for *twenty-eight years*.

I have no idea how much pornography I've bought and then destroyed. Before the days of always available Internet porn, I'd driven up to one hundred and forty miles *one way* to purchase or view pornography. Then I'd destroy it after using it for sexual fantasy and masturbation. I'd feel so guilty, which would deepen to an intense shame over time as my desire became a habit.

At a very young age, sex was becoming my most important need. It was also a sign of love to me. I had a hard time controlling my desire to turn fantasy into reality. I didn't make it through junior high as a virgin, and the first two years of high school were not good for several girls, or for me. As hard as I tried, the love and fulfillment I wanted was not coming from sex, yet I was so sure that it should.

At seventeen, I thought I'd found the answer to my problem. I heard about the love of God through Jesus Christ. I truly asked him to be my Savior. A lot of things changed for me. I became popular with my classmates. I became a high school Who's Who recipient. Still, I struggled to control my sexual desires. Only God knows how many times I asked him to take my sexual urges away.

Then I thought the next best answer had arrived: I met a Christian girl at a Bible study. I fell head over heels in love and spent the next two years with clenched teeth and white knuckles trying to control my sexual urges toward her as we waited for marriage. Well, there was no magic wand on the wedding night, or the years that followed either.

The answer to the struggle inside me was not found in the simple request for Jesus to be my Savior and it wasn't found in a wife. There was something wrong within which became even more complicated by marriage. The more I tried to control it and the more I bargained with God to help me control it, the more it controlled me. I was an addict who didn't want to face his addiction.

Giving Myself Over

In Ephesians 4:19, the Apostle Paul wrote, "Having lost all sensitivity, they have given themselves over to sensuality so as to indulge in every kind of impurity with a continual lust for more." The definition of the Greek word for sensuality is "a disregarding of accepted rules and standards, morally unrestrained, especially in sexual activities."[1]

This aptly defined my behavior and I wanted to stop, so I tried harder. I prayed harder. I went to a Bible college. I earned a Bachelor of Arts degree with a double major in theology and psychology. *Perfect. Now I know a whole lot of Bible stuff and some counseling skills to figure myself out, right?*

Nope! My obsessive/compulsive secret desire for pornography became even more secretive, and the fear of being caught produced adrenaline, which turned the addiction into something simultaneously physical and emotional. An old family ancestral saying of my mother's comes to mind: "The harder I try, the behinder I get."

On the outside, my family and I appeared quite normal and prosperous. No one knew the secret me. No one knew of the arguments my wife and I had about sex—except our children, because our fights had awakened them.

On the outside, I was a star performer. I had graduated college with honors and was awarded Who's Who in American Colleges and Universities. During my junior year of college, I had even become a pastor of a small church.

On the outside, I'd reply to a church member's, "How are you today?" with, "Great! Praise the Lord! It's a great day to be alive." Yet on the inside I'd be thinking, *If you only knew the thoughts I had last night or the things I did, you'd see to it that the Christian community would tar and feather me and leave me to die. I wish I could just die. God, can't you just take me home?*

Guilt and shame lined my entire interior being. My life was stuck in the cycle of addiction.[2] Acting out the addiction always brought on more shame and despair. Sometimes I'd just lie on the sofa for days and try to sleep my depression away. Then I'd do the only thing I knew to feel better: plan some type of sexual experience. During this planning I'd feel better. I'd even get excited about life. But when I would follow through and take the fantasy in my mind to sexual release, the impending despair would crash into me like no other force I know.

Yet I couldn't stop. I'd find a way to view porn, see a strip show, or create my own fantasy.

All my life, it was easy for me to want to be alone, to hide, and do something sexual, especially when conflict, stress, or anxiety arose. I believed that I deserved to be hurt, even abused. Using sex as medication was the only way I knew to feel better. Being at fault for everything that's wrong with anything, or anyone, seemed very normal.

After all, what did it matter? I'd think, *No matter how hard I try, they'll just leave me in the end, so don't trust anyone.* I was stuck in an immature childhood belief system that wasn't working in my adult life, yet I lived that way because it was all I knew. Nothing would change in my life or in my behavior unless I sought a new foundation. I needed to change my core belief system.[3] But instead of doing that, I tried one last option.

We moved away from the city to a small rural community and I went into the restaurant business. Just the act of moving to a safe place reveals how out of control my life had become. Our move eased my guilt, just a little, about the counterfeit Christian I was. Plus, I thought it would be easier to control my behavior where pornography wasn't available. But I was an addict, so I figured out ways to access porn. I'd drive anywhere between thirty to a hundred and forty miles to get it. Eventually it came to the small rural community anyway.

The county seat community of almost four thousand residents offered nearly every civic organization known to man. I was involved in most all of them over the years of my addiction, including several terms as the city's mayor. It was more and more difficult to hide my secrets. I was taking more risks. The fear of being found out increased the adrenaline rushes. My life was in a downward spiral. I was connecting with other sexually addicted people of the opposite sex, and some of those encounters were too close for comfort.

I was headed for a crash landing sometime soon.

So I packed up my paper prostitutes and headed to Trails End.

QUESTIONS

1. Do you have compulsive or obsessive habits?
   What are they?

2. Do you do any of these habits to escape the pressures of life or to make yourself feel better?

3. Have you tried to stop your problem but can't seem to?

4. Have you asked God to take your problem away but you still have it?

5. Have you felt guilty or shameful about the problem?

6. Do you feel like you let God down?

7. Is your problem costing you more than money?
   Is it affecting your health or your relationships, or causing more problems for you, your family, or your friends?

8. Have you ever wished you could die so you wouldn't have to fight this thing any more?

9. Are you ready to be honest about yourself and your problem?

CHAPTER 2
CROSSING YOUR RED SEA

The road from addiction to recovery is very similar to the journey the people of Israel undertook when they left slavery under the Egyptian Pharaoh in 1491 B.C. and trekked to the Promised Land. Today, the Promised Land is most of the eastern seaboard of the Mediterranean Sea, including present-day Syria, Lebanon, Jordan, part of Iraq, and on down to Israel. The Israelites arrived there in 1451 B.C. after *forty years* of wandering.

During their trying exodus, the Israelites consoled themselves by remembering that they'd been delivered from their bondage to Egyptian slavery. They came to believe in the God who was delivering them. They learned discipline, as well as how to trust God rather than their own dysfunctional, past thinking. They also had to learn rules, laws, and organization so chaos wouldn't govern their lives. Later in this book, we'll further discuss how these issues apply to a recovering addict's journey as well. For now, let's consider the most insurmountable circumstance they had to overcome.

Before Israel could even begin their journey to the Promised Land, they had to cross the Red Sea. Their Promised Land was a place of hope, contentment, peace, and freedom from the oppressiveness of slavery, but to get there the Israelites had to face an obstacle they could not overcome on their own. So God parted the waters of the Red Sea and Israel crossed over on dry land.

As an addict, you face a similar obstacle. It may not be a sea that can't be crossed by human effort, but it's every bit a barrier you haven't been able to overcome and cannot overcome on your own. You cannot move on to a life free from slavery to your addiction until you cross that barrier—and we all must overcome the same barrier.

Your Red Sea is your will.

The Red Sea of Your Will
How many times have you quit your addiction? How many times have you gone back to it?

In my case, I lost count. But "many, many, and many times" would sum up my answer.

You cannot move on to a better life until you cross this Sea of Will. This Sea is a place in your life of applying Steps 2 and 3 of the well-known 12 Steps used in so many addiction recovery programs:

- "Step 2: Came to believe that a power greater than ourselves could restore us to sanity."

- "Step 3: Made a decision to turn our will and our lives over to the care of God as we understood Him."

In other words, you must believe that God can do something in your life that you cannot (like parting a massive sea) and you must decide to turn your life and your will over to Him. You must also decide to not take control back once you encounter another obstacle. At every conflict or roadblock, or even with positive opportunities, we addicts often choose to go back to the familiar: our addiction.

I was tired of trying to control my addiction to no avail. I stood at my Red Sea. I looked behind me at years of addiction. I saw despair and felt an overwhelming weight of guilt and shame. The addiction always tricked me into thinking it would provide some comfort or fulfillment. Its end was always shame and pain for me and those around me.

I looked ahead and couldn't see anything on the other side of my Red Sea. I didn't know that place, a place where I wasn't in control. How could that even work? I didn't know the way or how I was going to get across, but I was very familiar with the bondage and slavery that lay behind me. I knew I couldn't say I was going to try or I was going to work at it. That had never worked.

Somewhere I'd heard that the will could be used in a healthy manner, so I took my first step in using my will in such a way. I made a statement of my will. I wrote it down. I said it out loud: "I will not go back. I will not look at pornography in any of its forms."

I was coming to believe.

In 1 Peter 5:6–7, the Apostle Peter wrote that if I would humble myself under God's mighty hand, he would lift me up in due time. I didn't like that "due time" part. But the barrier of my will had to be crossed. Trusting in God's will needed to become primary over trusting in my own will. But yielding my will?

I'll be vulnerable. Who's going to protect me? Who's going to see to it that my needs are met? This feels way too vulnerable. I'm going to die doing this!

Ah, I'm dying anyway.

From Ephesians 2:18–20, I reasoned that God has the power to raise the dead. I reasoned that God was on the other side of my Red Sea. I also knew from the Bible that God was in front of me and behind me. He was covering me. He had given his angels charge over me. He was not shaming me. Rather, he was inviting me to reconcile with him. He was promising to restore my life, to lift me up and cause me to live. He wanted only one thing from me: to turn my will and my life over to him.

AA slogans came to mind: "I'm sick and tired of being sick and tired." "If nothing changes, nothing changes." I knew I needed to change. I knew that my choice was either going back to the slavery of addiction or crossing the Red Sea of my will to an unknown place with an unknown future.

Many prayers of faith exist that talk about accepting Christ as Savior by turning our life over to him. Very few seem to ever include turning our will over to him also. For the first time in my life, I surrendered my will to God. I said, "I will follow you, Lord, wherever this goes. I will cross over, and I will follow and trust you for my every need."

I didn't know what awaited me on the other side, but I knew I had to get there.

The First Step

We cannot set ourselves right with the creator God of the universe. 2 Corinthians 5:20b–21 reveals this truth: "Be reconciled to God. God made him who had no sin, to be sin (a sin offering) for us, so that in him we might become the righteousness of God." That verse pairs well with Step 2 of the 12 steps: "Came to believe that a power greater than myself could restore me to sanity." To begin your journey from addiction to freedom, you must understand that the power to do so comes from God.

Addicts seek after many "powers" in their lives. Most all of them are obsessions that turn into addictions. In his letter to the Christ-followers in Rome, the Apostle Paul wrote,

> But now apart from the law the righteousness of God has been made known, to which the Law and the Prophets testify. *This righteousness is given through faith in Jesus Christ to all who believe.* There is no difference between Jew and Gentile, for all have sinned and fall short of the glory of God, and all are justified freely by his grace through the redemption that came by Christ Jesus. God presented Christ as a sacrifice of atonement, through the shedding of his blood—to be received by faith. He did this to demonstrate his righteousness, because in his forbearance he had left the sins committed beforehand unpunished—he did it to demonstrate his righteousness at the present time, so as to be just and the one who justifies those who have faith in Jesus (Romans 3:21-26, emphasis added).

Righteousness comes from God. He gives you this right-standing when you have faith in and believe in Jesus Christ. When you do this, you'll find yourself (in spite of yourself) justified in God's sight. Justified is a judicial term that means "to declare guiltless." *Really? God would declare* me *guiltless?* Yes, he would, no matter what you've done or are doing.

In Ephesians 6:14, Paul wrote, "Stand firm then, with the belt of truth buckled around your waist, with the breastplate of righteousness in place . . . ." In that day, the breastplate was comprised of two parts, a front and a back. You must choose to figuratively don that breastplate, which is to have faith and trust in Jesus Christ. When you do so, you will be clothed, covered, and surrounded by the right-standing God freely gives. You will be declared guiltless in his sight.

This great God has never changed in his endeavors to help his people. When Israel left their bondage in Egypt about 3,700 years ago, God went in front of them by day and by night.[4] Around 2,700 years ago, God went both before his people and was their rearguard.[5] Today, because of what Jesus accomplished on the cross, we are surrounded by his grace and made righteous in his sight. This is the good news.

I wanted this righteousness more than anything! I wanted to be right in God's eyes. I had so failed in all my attempts to please him. Everything I tried fell miserably short. I'd lived an idolatrous life. As a result of my addiction, my life was out of control and unmanageable. I was filled with guilt and shame. Yet there before me was the creator God offering me reconciliation, a restoration to favor in his sight, and the judicial proclamation of freedom. The gavel of God came down in my life and the proclamation was, "Guiltless!"

I learned this truth, from my head to my heart: "God was reconciling the world (including you and me) to himself in Christ, not counting men's sins against them" (2 Corinthians 5:19). The quiet voice that once told me, "Don't do it" when I was on the brink of suicide offered me more than a second chance. He offered me grace, forgiveness, and hope.

I came to believe that this God, this higher power, was the only power who could restore my life and do for me what I could not do for myself. I decided to trust him alone. In return, he reconciled me to himself and gave me right-standing in his sight.

He'll do that for you too.

The Secret to Crossing Over

To cross this great chasm to an unknown place of God's promise, restored sanity, healing, freedom, and life, you must be willing to expose your secrets. They may be shameful, but you cannot have your addiction and yield your will to God at the same time.

In Luke 16:13, Jesus memorably said, "No one can serve two masters. Either you will hate the one and love the other, or you will be devoted to the one and despise the other. You cannot serve both God and money."[6] Now, insert your addiction for the word "money." "You cannot serve both God and" drugs, or alcohol, or food, or gambling, or pornography, or you name it.

Part of crossing over is to start living in the truth about yourself. Telling what you have done in secret will free you from the shame you harbor inside and breaks the power the secret holds on your life. Much of the power that addiction has in your life stems from the secrets you hold. Secrets will cripple you emotionally and spiritually.[7]

Exercise care in where and to whom you expose your secrets. Not all places are safe or beneficial to do so. A recovery group or a skilled counselor in your field of addiction is my recommendation for such exposure. Coming clean doesn't give us as addicts the right to hurt or unduly upset innocent listeners.

One of my wrong places was my church's board. I used the "M" word and everything. That was twenty-four years ago, but I still remember that some people in the room even had their hands over their ears. I'm sure some of those older, conservative men would have been flogged by both their parents for using such words in church. I was making their ears bleed. I was giving too much information in the wrong place.

Another bad place to expose your secrets is to the town crier. This can result in more shame being dumped on you by well-meaning (and not-so-well-meaning) people. I never sexually abused any of my children, but because I'd divulged my secrets, my town crier started asking all their contacts if they thought I might have. I don't think I ever totally overcame that allegation, although I'm content to know that my children and I know the truth. You can't protect yourself against every rumor and you shouldn't try. Knowing the truth about yourself is more important, but speaking it in a safe environment to the right people is best.

Telling the truth about yourself will also lead to burning some bridges. Some friends may burn bridges with you, but I'm more advocating for *you* to burn the bridges between you and the dangerous people and places in your life. Even as you're reading these words, you probably already know which bridges you need to burn. They're the ones that lead you to the people and places where your addiction is enabled or even acted out. Leave no opening on this. Be firm enough to not leave a way back. Don't partially burn a bridge. I told every individual I had acted out my addiction with about my choice to *not* engage in it any more. In some cases, that ended friendships and relationships, but it was the best choice for me to make. I didn't need someone to help me walk backward through my Red Sea and to the slavery I'd just escaped.

In fact, I once belonged to a men's civic group where "extracurricular activities" like visiting strip clubs on out-of-town trips was the norm. Using sensitive terminology, I informed the group of my addiction and my unwillingness to attend such activities. In doing so, I gained the support of several other men within the group who were also in recovery. They knew how difficult the process was and vowed to stick with me on those trips in order to help occupy my free time away from home with healthy alternatives. Surprisingly, just a year later (and for the next decade) after I'd taken a stand, no one else took a trip to a strip club on those outings, as far as I knew. Through that, I learned how just one person taking a stand for what's right can hold a powerful influence over others.

As for places where pornography is accessible, or strip clubs dot the landscape, or lewd behavior reigns, all of China doesn't have enough assets to tempt me to cross their threshold any more. I will not go there. As an act of will given strength by God to do so, I don't allow myself to come within a mile of such temptations.

Burn the bridges to what provides the substance of your addiction. Be verbal about what you're doing and surround yourself with those who will hold you accountable to your decision. The major supplier of pornography in my community was a gas station that only survived because of its high volume of porn sales. I informed the manager of my addiction and that I wouldn't be coming in any more. I also informed all of my friends of my addiction and told them I couldn't have anything to do with porn. I asked them to hold me accountable.

When you perform this exercise in specifically identifying your secret sin, you will come to know exactly what you're leaving behind. You may not know everything you need to leave behind, but that's all right. There are other places in the journey where you'll be able to leave more harmful things behind.

For now, naming your addiction, speaking the secrets you carry, and refusing to engage the people and places that support your addiction is a great start.

Set your foot on the other shore, the place where you'll begin to trust God, and let the sea close in and drown the way back. Don't be afraid. I've been there, on that bank, and so many other people have made that same journey.

From one bank to the other, you're not alone.

Don't look back.

What awaits you is a most great adventure.

God's Promises on Your Journey

During my journey from addiction to freedom, I clung to God's promises like an infant does his blanket. This great God whom I trust makes promises that never fail. He promises to go before you, be with you, never leave you, and never forsake you (Deuteronomy 31:8). He will always keep these promises. Even when you think he's not around—especially then—trust that he is, because he *is*. Never forget the benefits of this trust. He forgives all your sins, heals all your diseases (and addictions), redeems your life from the pit, crowns you with love and compassion, satisfies your desires with good things, and renews your life (Psalm 103:2–5). These are great promises. Hang on to them.

Always remember that God does not treat you as your sins deserve. He desires to free you from your bondage in order that you may live a life of serenity and peace. Coming to believe that a power greater than yourself exists requires faith, otherwise known as a firm conviction. Make it your firm conviction to trust God's promises for you. Open your Bible and explore. God will give you personal promises. Write them down. Memorize them. "My eyes are ever on the Lord, for only he will release me from the snare" (Psalm 22:15). This is how to follow a power greater than yourself.

The Bible is my primary resource for promises. However, I've also read many books on my addiction. I encourage you to do the same. You can discover many promises that will give you hope and a concept of your recovery destination from people who have walked your walk. I especially like books that have recovery stories, like *The Big Book of Alcoholics Anonymous*. These stories give us hope for our journeys.

Other people will help you hold onto promises as well. A friend and pastor once gave me a promise that took all the faith I could muster to even write down. I'd just crossed my Red Sea and was metaphorically sitting on the far shore of a place I'd never been. He told me that if I would stick to recovery, apply the 12 Steps to my life, and trust and follow God, the very thing that had attracted me and dominated my life would become disgusting. He promised that I would come to see it for the evil that it was and is. I couldn't comprehend that then, but I wrote it down as a promise that could become true on my journey.

I received many promises and a lot of hope from my recovery group. Being on the far bank of the sea is like being in a recovery group, except you don't have a pin yet. You may have a day or week of abstinence from your addiction, and it's hard to comprehend folks getting a one-month sobriety pin or, harder yet, a six-month or one-year pin. *Is that possible? Are they telling the truth?* You'll find that they are, and you will gain great hope from your new, true friends. They will become friends who will wrap their arms of unconditional acceptance around you and gracefully encourage you on your recovery journey. Search for and find such a group. They will become priceless to you.

Lastly, allow me to share one more big promise: on the other side of the great adventure is a place where you will never fall. *Never fall?* Yes, never fall.

Back then, I didn't comprehend this concept. Never is a long time. I wrote down 2 Peter 1:3–11 and I read it often, in wonder and in hope, that it could be true for me:

> *His divine power has given us everything we need for a godly life* through our knowledge of him who called us by his own glory and goodness. Through these he has given us his very great and precious promises, so that through them you may participate in the divine nature, having escaped the corruption in the world caused by evil desires.
>
> For this very reason, make every effort to add to your faith goodness; and to goodness, knowledge; and to knowledge, self-control; and to self-control, perseverance; and to perseverance, godliness; and to godliness, mutual affection; and to mutual affection, love. For if you possess these qualities in increasing measure, they will keep you from being ineffective and unproductive in your knowledge of our Lord Jesus Christ. But whoever does not have them is nearsighted and blind, forgetting that they have been cleansed from their past sins.
>
> Therefore, my brothers and sisters, make every effort to confirm your calling and election. *For if you do these things, you will never fall*, and you will receive a rich welcome into the eternal kingdom of our Lord and Savior Jesus Christ (emphasis added).

This passage speaks about the higher power, God, who comes to us when you trust in him. "His divine power has given us everything we need for a godly life" (2 Peter 1:3). Notice: *his* power, not yours. Through his power and promises, you can be godly and escape the corruption caused by evil desires. Also notice that it's faith on your part (your firm conviction), but the power and responsibility for honoring his promises is God's part.

And where this passage says if we add goodness, knowledge, self-control, perseverance, godliness, brotherly kindness and love to our faith, you will never fall? I desperately wanted that. I was so sick and tired of fighting the same old fight with the same shameful outcome.

I hope some of these promises help you get up, face the great adventure of life without your addiction, and continue your journey far beyond your Red Sea crossing. Take baby steps, one day— even one moment—at a time. Don't look back, hold on to God, and trust his immense promises. He is faithful to them and to you. And after you've learned to take those steps day-by-day, eventually those days add up to six months, or a year, or five years, or ten, or the rest of your life.

You can do that.

God's promise.

QUESTIONS

The Red Sea of Your Will

1. What is your Red Sea?

2. Write down a statement(s) of your will in regard to your addiction/sin.

3. Are you ready to surrender your will to God? How would you put that in writing?

The First Step

1. What does "justified" mean?

2. How do you put on the breastplate of righteousness?

3. What happens to you when you put on the breastplate of righteousness?

4. God has provided the way to reconcile with you. Are you ready to reconcile with him? Why or why not?

The Secret to Crossing Over

1. What is your secret(s)?

2. Who are you going to tell about your secret(s)?

3. How would you describe burning a bridge in your life?

4. Who are some people you need to burn a bridge with?

5. What are some places you need to burn a bridge with?

God's Promises on Your Journey

1. What are some of God's promises for you from this chapter?

2. Do you know some other promises of God? Write them down.

3. Where else can you find more promises of God or about a life free from addiction?

4. What is faith? Will you place that faith in these promises?

CHAPTER 3
THE GREAT ADVENTURE

I once took a forty-question self-examination test on sexual addiction. I thought I'd done petty well on the test because I'd answered "maybe" only a couple of times. Then I read the instructions: "Be deeply honest with yourself and look for *any possible way* the question could pertain to your life."

The first time through, I had looked for ways the questions didn't really fit me or my circumstances. I gave myself an out on nearly every question because it didn't strictly apply to me. But the instructions had told me to do otherwise. I was supposed to have been so honest that I should have implicated myself if there was any way possible to do so. I took the test again.

I think the only question I passed was if I were male or female.

In that moment, I finally learned what it meant to be brutally honest with yourself.

I wasn't sure I ever wanted to do it again.

But then I was reminded of Reinhold Niebuhr's famous Serenity Prayer, a long-used and oft-repeated prayer of addicts across the nation: "God, grant me the serenity to accept the things I cannot change, the courage to change the things I can, and the wisdom to know the difference. Living one day at a time, enjoying one moment at a time; accepting hardship as a pathway to peace; taking, as Jesus did, this sinful world as it is, not as I would have it; trusting that you will make all things right if I surrender to your will; so that I may be reasonably happy in this life and supremely happy with you forever in the next. Amen."

This part of the journey—seeking the courage to change the things you can—is uncharted territory in your life. It certainly was in mine. As addicts, we've spent a lifetime trying to get what we want by manipulating others and scheming to have our deepest unmet desires fulfilled. As an addict, you're a master con artist, but you've only succeeded in deceiving yourself. You must change the only thing you can change: yourself. Such change requires great courage because you have to learn how to be brutally honest about yourself.

Personally, my courage comes from God through his Word. I have a pack of Bible verses that speak to my addiction and recovery. The first verse I memorized, and have probably spoken more than any other, is 2 Timothy 1:7: "For God did not give us a spirit of timidity (weakness), but a spirit of power, of love and of self-discipline." The second verse in my pack is Ecclesiastes 7:8–9: "The end of a matter is better than its beginning and patience is better than pride. Do not be quickly provoked in your spirit, for anger resides in the lap of fools (morally deficient)."

I don't just memorize these verses. Rather, I contemplate these verses and think about how they apply specifically to my life, not someone else's. When verses like these seep into your soul, you'll be met with its truth the next time you think about acting out your addiction. You will be encouraged by the fact that "God has not given me a spirit of weakness, but of power, love and of self-discipline." Then you'll be able to say to yourself and to God, "I will not go back. The end of this will be better than right now. God, help me to trust this new way of thinking."

These two verses gave me courage to face myself and continue taking the right steps away from my addiction and toward the freedom found in recovery. Feel free to use these verses too, but be open to God providing particular verses just for you. God is living and active in your recovery. His eyes actually search throughout the earth, looking for someone to help. That verse even says God searches "to strengthen those whose hearts are fully committed to him" (2 Chronicles 16:9).

If you want his help, he's looking to help you, to strengthen you, and to give you courage. The creator God yearns to restore your life to sanity. This fact ought to give you great courage for the next step in your adventure, a place where you'll need more courage than you've ever had before: a fearless self-examination.

Fearlessly Examine Yourself

Step 4 of The 12 Steps asks addicts to make "a searching and fearless moral inventory" of themselves. The Apostle Paul calls it "taking every thought captive" (2 Corinthians 10:5). Either way, to achieve victory where you've constantly failed, you're encouraged to take a deep and honest look at yourself.

Obviously, taking *every* thought captive will require a long time, but you just have to start. You don't have to complete the task all at once. To begin your fearless moral inventory, list your character defects, but be sure to list your positive characteristics too. This is an "I am who I am," cold, hard fact list about yourself.

Start with the obvious: your bottom-line, acting out addictive behavior. For me, it was viewing pornography and spending inordinate amounts of time in sexual fantasy and self-stimulation. Your addiction may also be sex-related, or it could center on alcohol, drugs, gambling, or food. List exactly what you are powerless to stop no matter its title. After listing your addictive behavior, move to your character defects. You may list more in time, but for now just make a rudimentary start.

A partial list of my character defects included self-centeredness, a fear of abandonment, anger, pride, self-righteousness, self-pity, defensive behavior, and blaming. I noticed a negative pattern in my life. When stress or confrontation occurred, these character flaws would manifest themselves in my behavior. When relational conflict occurred, I was compulsively drawn to my addictive behavior. Sometimes I would even create conflict in order to have an excuse to do my addictive behavior.

I trusted God to help me undertake my fearless self-examination. I read my Bible daily and asked God to show me where my thoughts were not his and where I needed to change my thinking. Particular verses would seem to stand out on the page, like I really couldn't go past them. I'd think on those verses often and would soon see how that verse was a way of thinking that applied to some flaw on my list. I thank God that this was a slow process. If we knew our flaws all at once, I don't think we could bear it.

The hardest thing to do was asking my family, and co-workers for help. These folks may not know anything about your particular addiction, but you have been revealing your true character to those living in close proximity to you for a long time. Some of their words may sting. Its time for fearlessness, don't retaliate, listen.

I also asked for feedback from my recovery group and my sponsor. Their input was invaluable. I was fortunate to develop a close friend in recovery. I was driving eighty miles one way to a recovery group. I learned that another man was also coming from a long distance. We chose to meet at a part-way point so we could ride fifty miles of the journey together. Every Monday for three years, we had a recovery meeting both before and after the actual recovery meeting. We were a great help to each other.

A recovery group and a skilled counselor can help you identify character defects. These are primary places where you can openly discuss your character defects without judgment. But when I was first presented with that option, I hesitated. I didn't want to openly discuss my character flaws. *Are you kidding?*

My prior experience with sharing so bluntly was that such admissions would be used against you in whatever way possible and for as long as possible. Back in the 90s during my early recovery years, the church was one place *not* to admit "the exact nature of our wrongs," the fifth step of The 12 Steps. But I did admit the exact nature of my wrongs to my church. Unfortunately, the people of that church, where I'd been attending for many years, seemed to push me away. Still I stayed, and all because of one man.

As I forlornly walked into a Sunday service one week, I almost passed a pew several rows ahead of the back row. A lone man occupied that pew. I didn't know the man then, but I knew of the man. From infancy, his children had sat in that pew with him and his wife. His children were now grown and had moved away. He was waiting to see his wife again some day in the heavenly realms. He was a lone man alone.

He motioned for me to come and sit by him. As I sat, he gestured from one end of the pew to the other and said, "This pew has always been reserved for sinners. You are welcome here with me." His unconditional acceptance is why I stayed. I loved that man. He has since gone to see his wife. I still strive to be a man of his character. We all should. We should all be that one man or woman who beckons as he does: "You are welcome here with me."

If recovery groups or rock-solid small groups consisted of people like this man, addicts like me wouldn't have to fear admitting the exact nature of our wrongs. We could openly share our lists with other people who view themselves as sinners, not saints. We could belong to churches comprised of people in the process of becoming better and willing stand alongside each other to encourage and support one another. The church I am a part of has many people like this today, and I am grateful I stayed.

Still, regardless of where you share, fearlessly confronting yourself in the presence of others is a daunting task. I remember my fear as I first started to share my innermost being at my recovery group meetings. Yet I also remember how quickly my fear dissipated as others shared their stories and I began to identify with them. I was no longer alone among judgmental critics or well-meaning advice-givers. I was with helpful peers on a similar journey of progress in the face of our common imperfections. I'd found true fellowship in a place where I was built up instead of torn down. Not one word of discussion in those meetings ever became gossip. For the first time in my life, at thirty eight years old, I was learning to trust another human being emotionally and spiritually.

Should this dynamic be part of the organized church? Of course! I think it is—in some places. I believe Christ-followers in recovery have much to offer the local church in this regard. Becoming comfortable in sharing our innermost, secret selves and identifying our character defects presents the church with a picture of who we are and why we behave the way we do.

But you can't just reveal yourself and expect others or your circumstances to adapt to your confessions. The only way your behavior will change is if you change the way you think. Relying on God, you must allow your character defects to be removed. Then, you must replace your dysfunctional belief system with a healthy belief system.

Let me tell you what I did to rebuild my belief system. I truly believe it will work for you too.

Rebuild Your Belief System

"Do not conform any longer to the pattern of this world, but be transformed by the renewing of your mind" (Romans 12:2). To be transformed is to undergo a metamorphosis, a marked or complete change of character, appearance, or condition. To be renewed is to be renovated.

In a house renovation, some things are removed and replaced with new parts. General cleanup and repairs happen. The goal is to bring the house back to an as-new condition. When a renovation is complete, the homeowner stands at a distance with their before pictures and marvels at the transformation that has taken place. This is exactly what you want to accomplish through your recovery journey.

The goal is a renovation of your belief system that results in a complete change of character, appearance, or condition. There will come a time in your renovation process that you may look the same physically, but you will not be the same person inside because, in many ways, you will not think or believe the way you once did. Consequently, you will no longer behave the way you once did. Your new behavior will reflect your new way of thinking.

Christ-followers have a tremendous advantage in this transformation and renewal process over any other higher power chosen outside the God of Judeo-Christian history. However, you must choose to take God at his word. In 2 Corinthians 10:3–5, the Apostle Paul states, "For though we live in the world, we do not wage war the way the world does. The weapons we fight with are not the weapons of the world. On the contrary, they have *divine power* to demolish strongholds. We demolish arguments and every pretension that sets itself up against the knowledge of God, and we take captive every thought to make it obedient to Christ" (emphasis added).

The words "divine power" should get your attention. They sure received mine. Strongholds are fortifications of error or vice, like your ingrained habits of addictive behavior and the character defects and beliefs which drive them. But we've been given divine power to pull down or demolish those beliefs and behaviors that bring harm to our lives. Now, that *has* to get your attention. With his divine power, you can change your belief system and behaviors.

God has given you an immensely helpful tool for your renovation project: a sword. "Take up . . . the sword of the Spirit, which is the word of God" (Ephesians 6:17b). When this letter was written to the Ephesian church, a literal sword bearer had the power over life and death. The executioner and the soldier in authority had that power. Spiritually bearing the sword of God's Word offers you life-and-death power over your emotions, mind, and behavior.

God's Word also provides the power to shape your life and the strength to maintain its new course. The use of God's Word as power to transform a human life was practiced long before the New Testament too. A thousand years or so prior to Jesus's birth, the nation of Israel's King David said to God, "I seek you with all my heart, do not let me stray from your commands. I have hidden your word in my heart that I might not sin against you" (Psalm 119:10–11). To take up the sword is to contemplate, memorize, and apply God's Word to your life. The power to renew and transform is found in the Word of God, our higher power. His word is living and active. It penetrates deep within and rebuilds us from the inside. His Word is our divine power, a power that can raise the dead.[8]

The next step of your renovation project is to use the divine power of God's Word to rebuild your belief system. Take your character defect list and lay it alongside the truth of God's Word. Get an easy-to-understand Bible. I use the *New International Version*. Use a concordance, which will help you locate certain words and topics in the Bible so you can learn the true meanings of those words or topics by reading the full context. Ask God to help you. If you're stuck, ask for help from a Christian support group or from a Christ-follower in a recovery program. A pastor who knows something about recovery should be able to help you get started in reading and applying the Bible too. I personally read my Bible a lot while asking God to direct me. Here are some examples of how this worked for me.

I quickly learned that it was dangerous to tread near the prostitute and the adulteress. Just read Proverbs 6 and 7. The bottom line is that these tempting women will reduce you to a loaf of bread and their homes are but highways to the grave. (The same can be said of men who tempt women, as statistics show that the prevalence of Internet pornography is also increasing porn addiction among women.) Pictures and movies are no exception to the living form either. They are both equally destructive.

I learned a lot from reading recovery books on sexual addiction and going to professional counseling. I concluded that if I did anything sexual outside a long-term, committed relationship, it would be addictive sex. This was evidenced by the fact that I spent more time with my paper and video prostitutes than I did pursuing God. The knockdown, knockout Bible verse that brought truth and clarity to my thinking was Luke 16:13: "No servant can serve two masters. Either he will hate the one and love the other, or he will be devoted to the one and despise the other. You cannot serve both God and money." In that verse, I replaced "money" with the word "pornography." You can put whatever addiction you want in place of the word money and not change the meaning of this part of the Word of God.

Every time the thought of porn came to my mind, I'd say or think this verse. I said the verse so many times that I found myself thinking about it in my dreams. The power of this particular word of God halted my thoughts about porn. It also extinguished my dreams about porn and eventually erased them. I had other verses, but this one became very powerful in my life.

Think about it: you cannot be a servant to two bosses, and especially to two opposing bosses. You're going to hate and despise one and will love and be devoted to the other. While I was devoted to porn and my addictive behavior, I could not love and be devoted to God at the same time. At best my life was hypocritical, like an actor on a stage portraying one person yet in fact being another.

We addicts rationalize many things so we can justify our addictions. Our dysfunctional thinking tells us we can do whatever we want. Somehow we believe we're above the so-called normal rules of life. The difficulties we sometimes face are that *other* people don't line up with what we want. If they would *just do what we want them to*, then everything would be all right. If they don't, we tend to get angry—at least I did.

Anger was another of my character defects, so I set out to read and learn about anger from the Bible. I know some scholarly theologians are going to point out that Jesus was angry when he turned over tables in the temple. I'm sure he was, but I didn't need any more rationalizations to help me continue venting my anger. We can certainly be angry and not sin, but my problem was that when I got angry, someone usually got hurt (including me).

This was made all too apparent when my son, an outstanding high school athlete at the time, brought his friends over to our house to watch gameplay footage from a recent football game of theirs. One of the guys didn't want to watch it because they'd lost. But I overheard my son say, "It's not about the game. You have to hear my dad and the things he says in the background."

It wasn't pretty. If my words had been bullets, the referees would have all been dead. I hope that video's lost forever. I wish I would have started sooner in my life in the process of renewing my mind to healthier thoughts—even for referees.

Consequently, I put two verses in my memory pack: "The end of a matter is better than its beginning, and patience is better than pride. Do not be quickly provoked in your spirit, for anger resides in the lap of fools" (Ecclesiastes 7:8–9). Many times I was the fool. Another verse that brought divine power in changing my anger responses is Proverbs 16:32: "Better a patient man than a warrior, a man that controls his temper than one who takes a city."

God only knows how many times I said those verses to myself over the years. They are firmly in my mind now and are a part of my new thinking. I'm not perfect in controlling my anger, but the difference from twenty-four years ago is a definite transformation.

Still, my defensive character traits run deep. God has brought me a long way, but I continue to pursue knowing the total power of Proverbs 16:32. Nothing astounds me more than Jesus's characteristics in his last days before he was crucified, like 1 Peter 2:23: "When they hurled their insults at him, he did not retaliate; when he suffered, he made no threats. Instead, he entrusted himself to him who judges justly." Jesus didn't retaliate or threaten, even in the face of injustice. He simply let go to the fact that God knows the truth and that's sufficient for him. This is certainly a serene way to live life.

Are you getting the idea? There's no magic wand or shortcut to changing your belief system. It's hard work. But if nothing changes, then all remains the same. I encourage you to go deep in this process. Dive beyond the surface. Get professional help specific to your addiction. Even better, seek a counselor who is educated and in recovery from your same addiction. They can help you identify your core beliefs that trigger and drive your behaviors.

Search for the best counselor and pay the money he or she may cost you. Try to find a shepherd who has walked the pasture and not just someone who thinks they know something. I believe my advice pertains to all addictions. After all, if you're having heart problems, you'll want visit a physically fit cardiologist, not an obese one—or even worse, a proctologist.

My Counseling Experience

I learned the hard way first. One pastor and several professional counselors I visited I now know were sex addicts themselves. When I made the commitment of time and money for the best I could find, I really started to understand my core beliefs and why I behaved like I did. Five years into my recovery, I began driving 145 miles, one way, for the best counselor I could find, Mark. He guided me deeply inside myself. My wife came with me for a short time but soon refused to keep attending. I continued counseling by myself for the next seven years, going once a month with some breaks.

Twelve years into my recovery and thirty-two years into my marriage, my recovery was progressing wonderfully, but my marriage continued to degrade. It was a long process in its development, but I truly had come to believe that I was responsible for *all* of our marriage problems. I would repeatedly sit and listen to my wife's list of all the ways I had wronged her. Sure, I had wronged my wife in some ways. Taking responsibility for my part wasn't the problem. Her list was now thirty-two-years long and offered no opportunity for any resolution. She was convinced that a repeated airing of the list was the only way she could heal from all the damage I had done to her.

I believed her. I had settled in on accepting the blame for everything wrong in our marriage.

I remember a question my counselor once asked me: "What in the world happened in your family, while growing up, that makes you think you deserve to be abused?"

I told him of the childhood abuse I'd experienced which I've already recounted in this book.

The counselor followed my answers with just about the same line every time: "You've felt that way before, haven't you?"

I soon discovered why I was connected, loyal, supportive, and even helpful to people who were dangerous, shaming, and exploitive. I learned that my actions and reactions were called a "trauma bond," which means being connected, i.e., loyal, helpful, or supportive, to people who are dangerous, shaming, or exploitative.[9]

I'd always believed that I deserved it or had it coming because that had always been verbalized at me. My mother made statements like, "Shame on you!" and would often ask, "What did you do to make your brother so mad at you?" I checked my memory on this by asking my brother his recollection of these events. His responses were difficult for me. It was like going back fifty years.

My brother still viewed me as the one at fault in some way. His wife even voiced agreement. Obviously, there had been discussions as to our childhoods, and I was viewed as the little problem child that had just gotten what he had coming. Most of my life, I tried to gain the approval of this brother, but to no avail. I thought the reasons I couldn't were always my fault. Getting my brother to understand his past or present wasn't my goal; understanding mine was. I was learning the origins of why I had carried some dysfunctional beliefs into my adult life. I was now with a marriage partner who was emotionally unavailable and fit the same patterns with which I'd grown up.[10] I was desperately trying to win her approval and make her available by somehow earning it, even though all the evidence demonstrated my attempts weren't working. That recipe for disaster was working the same as it had with my brother.

I wrote an entry in my journal on June 14, 2004 that at 10:30 a.m. while in Dr. Mark's counseling office, "A light bulb came on in my head. I had a lot of wishful thinking and an addict's fantasy that everything will just work out." I was learning why I couldn't stand up for myself. Sure, I could yell and be angry, but I couldn't set boundaries to protect myself or enforce them. Who would I pick to be in a close, intimate relationship? I was sure I'd pick someone unavailable every time. Even my fantasies about women had all been about women who were unavailable.

I believed I could do or attempt to do things that would change another person's beliefs or actions. I felt responsible for other people's behaviors and feelings. I would compromise my own wants and beliefs to meet the demands of others. My fear and anxiety permitted me to tolerate and allow abuse and to not enforce, or even have, boundaries. These character defects led me to isolation or hiding out until it was safe to come out. My fears immobilized me—a pattern I had lived since being a young boy. If I were to ever have a healthy marriage, or any healthy, close relationships, this pattern would have to be torn out and rebuilt.

But in so doing it would change all of my relationships and most of my life.

I studied about betrayal bonds and emotional unavailability.[9,17] It was as though these authors had written their books specifically about me. I turned my anxiety over to God. He promised me in 1 Peter 5:6–11 that he would lift me up in due time and after a little while he would restore me and make me strong, firm, and steadfast. I gave my fear to God and he delivered me from my fear.[11] I took Psalm 91 seriously and made God my refuge and fortress. His promise for doing so is to save me and become my protector. I will no longer live in fear because the creator God of the universe will rescue me, guard me, lift me up, answer me, be with me, and satisfy me.

During the eleven years following that June morning and doing what Dr. Mark told me I would have to do ("Practice, practice, practice."), a new pattern emerged.

I have boundaries.

I do not have relationships with unavailable people.

I don't isolate myself in fear until I think it's safe to come out.

I do not use sex as stress relief.

I have no sex outside of the long-term committed relationship I am in with my wife.

I can have and maintain healthy relationships.

I can still have a reaction to an angry outburst. I'll freeze up for a bit, but I will stay in the relationship and work for resolution—in a healthy relationship that is. If it's not healthy, I don't bother. I know from my new belief system that it would be pointless.

I can't change anyone except me, and my change has been through a lot of hard work and the power of God in my life. God is in the human renovation business. He can transform your life if you choose to actively participate in changing your belief system by using the divine power of his Word to replace defective learning, beliefs, and behavior.

And also if you "practice, practice, practice."

Trust God

Put on the helmet of salvation. This piece of armor is a saving deliverance. To wear the helmet of salvation is to believe the gospel or "good news" of Jesus Christ. Romans 10:9-10 states it plainly: "If you confess with your mouth, 'Jesus is Lord' and believe in your heart that God raised him from the dead, you will be saved. For it is with your heart that you believe and are justified, and it is with your mouth that you confess and are saved." Putting this helmet on requires that you take it into your hands, place it on your head, *and leave it on.*

I thought I'd done this at seventeen. I confessed with my mouth, but I didn't follow the believe-in-your-heart requirement. "Heart belief affects your mind, emotions and will."[12] Judging by my actions after the time I thought I had put on the helmet of salvation, my will hadn't been changed by my verbal confession.

I had to ask myself a question: what does God ask of me? The answer has been there since nearly the beginning of recorded biblical history: respect him, walk in his ways, love him, serve him with all your heart and soul, and observe all of his words for your own good.

I do not mean that we have to work for or earn salvation. Salvation is by God's grace, a free gift. Embracing the good news of Jesus Christ is to realize you can do nothing to save yourself from the consequences of your sins. Jesus paid the consequences for all of us. Putting on the helmet of salvation is to guard and protect your mind with the fact that your saving and deliverance is a *gift* from God through Jesus Christ. When you embrace this truth and figuratively wear it, your mind, emotions, will, and behaviors will change. I walk in God's ways, not because I have to, but out of love and respect for all he has done for me—and because it's for my own good.[13]

Whom do I trust? I trust in the Lord God and him alone. For me, trusting God means to *keep* the helmet on, to *not* return to the idol of my addiction. Trusting God means to fix his Word in my heart and mind and let them direct my thoughts and behaviors. This is a place of tunnel vision, where the rubber of belief hits the road of real life. Trusting God is not changing my mind next week, next month, or whenever it suits me. Trusting God means that when the going gets tough, I will *still* choose to live by God's Word, and not because I have to, but because my life will be completely better if I do.

I knew I would be tested in this area. I knew I'd be tempted to go back to what had previously comforted me. You will be too. Evil never wants to see deliverance. But God does, so he provides help. In Psalm 33:18–22, King David let us know that when we respect God and put our hope in his unfailing love, God's eyes are watching so he can deliver us and get us through difficult times. When we wait in that hope, he becomes our help and our shield. 2 Chronicles 16:9 puts it this way: "For the eyes of the lord run to and fro throughout the whole earth to show himself strong on behalf of those whose heart is loyal to him."[14] Now, isn't that something? The God who created all we see and know of the universe is standing by, looking for the chance to *help us*, if we trust in him, with all of his strength and power. There is no other power in the universe except the creator God who promises this, follows through with his promise, and actually delivers.

I didn't decide to trust God because I was some theological genius. Yes, I graduated college with honors (and other accolades of self-sufficiency), but that just got in the way of trusting anything more than myself. I could do just about anything by myself. I was self-centered, and my self will ran wild. But I ended up crushed by the life I lived. I was humbled, not because of some great awakening, but because of where my addiction had taken me. I crashed into a bottom where I was not wanted by many of the people I knew. I was no longer respected. I was ashamed of my secret behavior now made public. I trusted God because he was the only one who still wanted me and was proclaiming his desire to help me.

In Isaiah 57:15, God says about himself, "For this is what the high and lofty one says—he who lives forever, whose name is holy: 'I live in a high and holy place, but also with him who is contrite and lowly in spirit, to revive the spirit of the lowly and to revive the heart of the contrite.'" "Contrite" means to be crushed, as in pulverized to dust. "Lowly" means to be afflicted, humble, and submissive. When I hit bottom, I surely passed these criteria.

The word "revive" in this verse means to cause to live.[15] The God who lives forever said he would come live with me and *cause me to live*. He would cause my spirit, my mind, my emotions, and my will to live. I trusted God by default. I had nowhere else to go. I called out to God, and he came to me and kept his word.

He will do this for you too.

Choose today to trust this great and awesome God who calls himself "I am."

Put on the helmet of salvation, and he will come to you and *cause you to live*.

Trust People

Trusting people is more difficult than trusting God. God keeps all of his promises and never fails. People don't always keep their promises, and we fail each other in countless ways. Jesus Christ did not entrust himself to people because he knew what was inside of them.[16] People are not God, and we should not expect them to be. We will never attain perfection in our life and we should not expect anyone else to either. Human relationships are faulty at best, yet we need them. God brings healing to our life through his Word *and* through people. We need to learn how to identify who these people are and nurture healthy relationships with them.

Some of these good relationships are more obvious than others. The first trust I extended to people was to my recovery group. As time progressed I became close friends with three men in that group. Our relationships grew based on developing trust in each other.

It wasn't until five years later that I extended trust to a counselor. He was a shepherd. He had walked the path before me and guided me with a gentle heart and a wealth of knowledge. I grew in trust, respect, and admiration for this man for the help and healing God was bringing to my life through him.

But there are also less obvious ways God brings good people into our lives. I owned and operated a restaurant during my recovery. At the close of a day shift, the dreaded private phone rang. No manager likes this kind of call: a key person had met with misfortune and wouldn't be coming in to work that night. (The person was all right in the long run, but had to quit that night.) I wished the employee well, but all the while I could only think of the circumstance's immediate effect on me. A very busy dinner hour was approaching, and I had no backup employees for that particular night—aside from myself. My head dropped to the counter. With twenty years in the business at the time, this wasn't completely unusual, but I was tired. I guessed I'd be pulling a double-shift yet again.

When I raised my head, a small, white-haired woman stood before me. I put on my best greeting face and asked, "How can I help you?" With a twinkle in her eye, she asked, "Are you hiring?"

My immediate reply was a thought rather than an answer: *we've never hired a senior citizen before.* However, the better part of me asked, "What experience do you have in the restaurant business?"

"My husband and I just moved to the area from a little south of here, to retire."

"What'd you do before you retired?"

"We owned and operated a restaurant just about like this one for, oh, twenty-seven years, I think."

Are you kidding me?

I didn't say that out loud. Instead, I asked, "Could you wait here for a minute?"

She nodded, and I turned to the store room. I came back to her and handed her a uniform.

"Can you start tonight?"

She gave me a big smile. "Sure thing, Boss."

She took the uniform and went to the ladies' room to change.

I have no doubt that that woman on that night was sent by God to encourage me when I felt more discouraged than I had been in a long time. In time, she also brought stability to our workforce and joy to everyone she worked with. To me, she even brought healing for the wounds of my childhood.

Corrine loved me as an emotionally available mother would love her son. In the years that followed I would be, in a sense, re-parented. Even the anger I'd held toward my mother for her unavailability and abandonment would subside and be covered in forgiveness. This former restaurateur, who just happened into my life, brought me loving-kindness, nurturing, sound motherly wisdom, and total unconditional acceptance.

God will bring people like Corrine to you too. Watch for them.

Unfortunately, some people who come into your life are not helpful. In fact, they can be downright hurtful.

A Broken Marriage Breaking

The best it gets for a marriage in recovery is to have the husband in recovery, the wife in recovery, *and* the couple in recovery. This was not the case in my marriage. We had one in and one out. This formula dissipates trust. Fourteen years into my recovery and with seven years of periodic counseling, my marriage continued to worsen. I was experiencing the risks that come with change.

Memorably, a friend of mine once told me, "There are always two sides to the paper, no matter how thin it is." This is so true of marriage relationships. I do not believe anyone should give up easily on their marriage.

My wife threatened divorce many times, which usually made me withdraw and become more compliant, which did little or nothing to improve our marriage. So I did the only thing I could do about changing the only thing I could: myself. I systematically began a process of eliminating the reasons my wife had against me for her to stay in our marriage. With outside guidance and accountability, I strived to identify and remove my wife's list of my character defects. During this concerted effort, the separate beds we slept in graduated to *five years* of living separate lives on separate floors in the same house. My wife gave me no indication of love, respect, or trust. The more change that occurred in me, the more distant we became. At best, we were just business partners. Most every personal discussion about restoring our marriage went from anger to rage in the rehearsal of past, unresolved conflict.

I was losing weight. I was only sleeping two to three hours per night. My health had been going down for years. At the time, I was consuming alcohol to cope, which wasn't helpful. For seven years, I had been deliberately trying to do everything I could do to save my marriage, but my wife could only see my past when she looked at me. She couldn't see me in the present. She couldn't see my changes.

The very process of healing that brought transformation to my life was dividing us. The more I changed, the more it seemed my wife tried to pull me back to where she thought "normal" should be. Her "normal" was now very dysfunctional and toxic to me. I believe my wife was committed to *not* change. She often stated, "I don't need to be fixed." I believe she viewed change as an exhibition of codependency toward me. Most probably, her position was based on our history with me as an addict. I saw no indication that she would ever budge from that history. I wanted no part of divorce. I was experiencing how the risk of change can bring a great divide between people.

Our marriage had become like a person with gangrene on their foot. They may not want to amputate their foot, but if they don't, they'll die.

The hardest thing I ever did was to visit an attorney to start the process of divorce. In the beginning, I had hoped it would shock my wife into wanting to go to counseling and save our marriage. It didn't. She got an attorney and the fight was on.

All of the reasons God hates divorce came out. Lies were told, blame was leveled, and friendships, family members, and lives were torn apart. I don't recommend divorce to anyone. It is, at best, the last resort.

I don't regret the years of effort I gave to save my marriage. I do regret that my wife chose not to participate in the process. I still believe God can bring healing to broken marriages, but both people have to want it and take individual responsibility for themselves. They have to ask the question, "What is it about *me* that needs to change?" When each person can honestly answer that question and engages in becoming the best they can be, *then* they can work on their relationship. With the willingness of both, and good help, nearly anything can be overcome. However, if you're experiencing physical abuse, follow Bryn C. Collins' advice: "Leave now and file charges."[17] Work on that relationship from a safe distance.

To Go Forward, Stop Going Back
As my life was being transformed, more than just my marriage ended. Many longstanding friendships faded as the changes in my character created differences in mutual interests. One person's character came into such sharp contrast with mine that to maintain that relationship would have brought me harm. This person actually argued with me that I should participate in what I knew to be sexually addictive, acting-out behavior. They were actually angry with me that I wouldn't comply. This person was outspoken and controlling. I ended any contact with them. I could not and would not flirt with my old addiction.

The wisest man to ever live, King Solomon, stated, "He who walks with the wise grows wise, but a companion of fools [the morally deficient] suffers harm" (Proverbs 13:20). "I will *not* go back" is something you (and I) will need to say many times in our new lives. Some people will always try to pull us off-course and backward. If they won't come with you or support you on your new healthy life journey, you must leave them behind, on the other side of your Red Sea. God will fill the vacancy with new and better relationships.

I had been so tied up in dysfunctional relationships for most of my life that I found myself yearning for healthy ones. I enjoyed great, new relationships with men. Some of these were with men in recovery, some were with older men in a civic organization, and some were from my church. I so wanted to know what it was like to be in a healthy relationship with a woman too.

Scared and shaking like a young teenager, I initiated phone conversations with several women our family had known for many years. These women knew my wife and me, but they no longer lived in the area, so I felt safe in calling them. One lady was going through a divorce, and the other two had been single for many years. The recurring conversations I had with two of the ladies, at times, were lengthy and, well, kind of amazing to me.

For the first time in a long time, I wasn't the enemy. I was participating in conversations that were edifying and mutual *with a female*. In our phone conversations I felt significant. I felt equal. These women truly cared about my thoughts, my life, who I was, and, maybe more importantly to me, who I was becoming. I was experiencing the kind of intimacy I'd only read about, and it was bringing hope and healing to me.

I eventually visited one of these ladies, painted part of her house, went to a movie with her and her grandchildren, and attended a church worship service together. In fact, my first date in thirty-two years with a female who was not my wife had nothing to do with sex. The conversations were filled with healthy intimacy. I wanted more of this. It felt like a warm shower on a freezing day.

Accusations of me having an affair ended my phone conversations. In defense of these ladies, nothing other than conversation ever occurred. Even though there was no evidence that my wife and I had any kind of a marriage for many years, the divorce was still not legally final. I could wait to pursue a new relationship with a woman. My wife had often told me I was incapable of having a relationship with any woman and that I was irreparable in that regard. But, something was happening inside my renewing belief system: I was learning that what she had told me about myself may not be right.

I continued to nurture my relationships with healthy men and Corrine. I was more determined than ever to leave unhealthy relationships and embrace healthy ones. According to Patrick Carnes, unhealthy intimacy in a relationship would exhibit non-nurturing behaviors.[18] Someone who is generally critical, controlling, or judgmental will try to talk you out of your feelings and will fail to help you when needed. An unhealthy person will be inattentive. They can't be present. They are undependable, avoid closure, and are emotionally unavailable.

Contrast unhealthy intimacy with Carnes' definition of healthy intimacy. The difference is quite inviting. In healthy intimacy, both people initiate within the relationship. They share in the relationship. Both are emotionally available. They listen, build trust, and work together to bring closure to problems. The relationship demonstrates responsiveness to the other's needs, and talks about dilemmas, thoughts, and feelings. It is mutually supportive, encouraging, has values, and both people are honest about their feelings. Each person is fully known.

When you develop healthy intimacy characteristics in your life and you place your feet into a healthy relationship, you will never want to go back to a sick and dysfunctional relationship. One is like motor oil and the other is like fresh spring water. Only one is good to drink—and they don't mix together at all.

Now I have a rule when deciding whom to trust: I will only extend trust to a person who demonstrates healthy intimacy as discussed above, period. God has brought many new people into my life. They bring healing and growth to me, and I bring that to them. We are companions on the journey. I trust them and they trust me.

People like this will come into your life. Watch for them. Embrace and nurture the healthy.

Setting Boundaries

Where is your destination? Where do you want to end up?

Webster's Dictionary defines a boundary as, "any line or thing marking a limit." Think of a guardrail on the side of a mountain road. Boundaries protect you and will keep you on track to reach your destination. If you stay inside the guardrails, you'll make it to your destination. If you go outside the guardrails, you'll endanger yourself and likely fail to reach your destination.

In addiction recovery, it seems as if everything is trying to pull you away from recovery and toward a culture that is out of control with addictions. The only way to maintain your recovery in this culture is to erect boundaries. You must establish which places you will and will not go. You have to set limits on what you will or will not eat, drink, or let your eyes see.

The fourth chapter of Proverbs contains great information on boundaries: "Take firm hold of instruction, do not let go; Keep her, for she is your life."[19] The instruction you have gained (or will gain) in recovery is your life. Hold on to it. Stick to it. Don't even look at the people still living in your addiction. Turn away and go on your way. Look straight ahead. Develop tunnel vision for the path of your recovery. Live in ways that are sure and proven to bring healthy living. Don't swerve to the right or left of that path.

Joshua 23:6–14 encourages the same never-swerving route. Under Joshua's leadership, the nation of Israel lived in great prosperity. He was nearing the end of his life when he wrote this passage as a reminder to Israel that not a single promise of God had failed. Why? Because of the boundaries they had lived within. So, Joshua reminds Israel to maintain their boundaries and not turn aside to the right or the left. He tells them that if they'll stay within those boundaries, they will continue to prosper.

But, Joshua warned that if they strayed outside of those boundaries, what they pursued would become whips on their backs and thorns in their eyes. Ouch! What a description for our old addictive behaviors. The concept of whips on our backs and thorns in our eyes certainly paints a striking image of life in the grasp of addiction and its consequences. You must set boundaries to protect yourself.

Protecting Yourself with a Red Shield
We have crossed the Red Sea, and we know that the red blood of Jesus Christ has reconciled us to a relationship with God. Our shield could be no other color than red, and now is the time for you to pick up your shield. "Take up the shield of faith, with which you can extinguish all the flaming arrows of the evil one" (Ephesians 6:16, NIV).

Let's look at each of the significant words individually:

- Shield: in this context, shield refers to a large, oblong shield to be used as protection. The same Greek word is used in Acts 14:27 and 1 Corinthians 16:9 and translated "door." In John 10:7 and 10:9, the same word is translated as "gate," or seen as a means of entrance. Other interpretations of this word have interpreted it as a stone or other material employed to close a door way.
- Faith: belief, a firm persuasion, assurance, or firm conviction.
- Extinguish: Quench, hinder, or thwart.
- Flaming: Fiery, burn, test, or a distressful feeling.
- Arrows: missile, arrow, dart, spear or weapon. A word that is not in my English translation text but appears in the Greek text is "power."

- Evil one: Bad, unsound, evil, afflictive, wrongful, malignant, malevolent, wicked.

Following the above definitions, a very literal translation of Ephesians 6:16 would be, "Pick up the shield of your firm persuasion (in God's word), with which you can defeat and close the door on *all* the powerful weapons of the evil one."

Employing the shield of faith is how to set boundaries, but more importantly, it is the way you can enforce your boundaries. This enforcement cannot be overcome by anything outside of us. Jesus demonstrated how to use the shield of faith in Matthew 4:4, 4:7 and 4:10. When being tempted by Satan in the desert, Jesus was under intense pressure to step outside the boundaries of trusting God. When the Evil One was using all of his powerful weapons to pull Jesus off course, Jesus responded by quoting God's Word. He hid behind the shield, i.e., his firm conviction and persuasion in the truth of God's Word, and defeated the temptations of the devil. He closed the door on all of his evil power.

When you place God's Word into your mind, it will transform your thinking. Now, you must use those words and others as a shield of protection.

I have very rigid boundaries concerning pornography. I will not look at it in any of its forms. Hardcore and softcore are the obvious forms, but pictures intended to arouse sexual desire are all around us. I will not look at them. I will not let them into my mind. Temptations to do so will come for sure.

Some will come when you're alone, but remember that true character is demonstrated by what you do in secret. Inevitably, you will use the bathroom at someone else's house and there will be magazines featuring scantily clad bodies. Don't even entertain the thought. Look away and say, "No servant can serve two masters. Either he will hate the one and love the other, or he will be devoted to the one and despise the other" (Luke 16:13, NIV).

You may rationalize a bad choice when you're alone, or even in public when some person will actually say, "Come on, you can look at a little skin." The truth is that once you do, it's very hard to get it out of your recall memory. To such people I bluntly say, "I'm a recovering sex addict, and for me that would be like an alcoholic just having one drink." Then I say to myself, "The body is not meant for sexual immorality but for the Lord" (1 Corinthians 6:13b, NIV).

Temptations can so easily get us off track, even from the most unlikely of sources. I remember once talking about my temptations with a pastor. He casually said, "There's a fine line between lust and appreciation."

Ahh!

We Christians are so accustomed to walking the fence, or having one foot on each side of the guardrail, that we can't even recognize when we're doing it. Sometimes we rationalize that we're strong enough to do so. Here was a *pastor* telling me that I could walk *closer* to the line. He should know, right? Maybe not!

I said to myself, "Anyone who looks at a woman lustfully has already committed adultery in his heart" (Matthew 5:27, NIV). The truth of God's Word, hiding behind my firm conviction for its truth and its power in my life, has always stopped the desire to get too close or step over my boundaries. I believe our boundaries should be like walls you can't see through or step over. What I mean is that you should never flirt with your boundary. If you do, you'll fall.

Notice that I'm not saying these scriptures to people. We Christians have an unfortunate reputation for using the Bible as a club. The shield is not a club; it is protection. Use it to protect and empower yourself to stay within the boundaries you've set. I'm not saying that you can't say God's Word out loud—certainly, you can—but what you say ought to be for you, not the other person. Set firm boundaries to protect yourself.

God's Word has absolutes. As you find them, write them down and use them to reinforce your guardrails. The path we want to walk is "living by every word that proceeds from the mouth of the Lord" (Matthew 4:4). In the environment where you live, you will have to lead and not follow when it comes to setting boundaries. Most people, it seems, don't have any boundaries, or certainly don't talk about them much. In America, we all live in an addictive society. When you set boundaries, someone, maybe even a pastor, is going to attempt to take them down—or at least try to coax you to cross them.

In Galatians 5:16–25, the Apostle Paul gives a partial list of where to start with setting healthy boundaries. In his list you will find addictions like drunkenness, sexual immorality, hatred, envy, witchcraft, idolatry, and other issues. If you do not have boundaries to keep away from those things and you participate in them, they will becomes whips on your back and thorns in your eyes.

But when you have boundaries and stay on a path away from temptations, you'll experience the promise of love, joy, peace, patience, kindness, goodness, faithfulness, gentleness, and self-control. Now, that doesn't require a lot of thought as to which is a more serene way of life. God's Word is absolute in Galatians 6:8: "The one who sows to please his sinful nature, from that nature will reap destruction." Destruction means erosion or deterioration. Living outside of healthy boundaries brings a painful deterioration. Anyone who has hit the bottom will agree.

With twenty-four years in recovery, I still have boundaries. I always will. I employ them everywhere. I keep them up at work, home, civic groups, and at church. There are some things you expect and can prepare for, but you need to be prepared for the unexpected. For a sex addict in recovery, you must anticipate dealing with inappropriate dress at the shopping mall, but you'll also get blindsided by the same problem at church. It is a mind-bender, but we shouldn't expect that all church attendees have both oars in the water when it comes to healthy boundaries.

As recovering addicts, we are the leaders in this regard. Lead by your example, firm in your conviction yet clothed in the grace God has given you. I will never budge on my bottom-line addictive behavior boundaries. Why would I want to? Without boundaries, all I experienced was bondage. I had whips on my back, thorns in my eyes, and a continuous deterioration in all aspects of life. With walls erected and the shield of faith to enforce them, I found freedom.

So will you if you are ardently loyal to the great adventure of the recovery journey.

Ardent Loyalty

I had no clue what "ardent" meant for the longest time. Years ago, a church leader was being insistent that I be a part of his men's study group. This wasn't a bad request in itself. However, by this time I was remarried. Because we're both in a second marriage and certainly do not want to repeat past mistakes, we set proper boundaries for our marriage, like how many activities we'd do apart from each other. We have a boundary that we will only attend small groups or Bible studies we can both attend.

When I explained this to the church leader (who only attended men's groups), he hesitated and then told me he appreciated my fierce loyalty to my wife. I told him thank you, not because I was following good communication principles, but because I thought I was being paid a compliment. When I got home, I looked up "fierce." I was hopeful for some good feelings and to be able to pat myself on the back. Well, the word means "a violently cruel nature, savage, uncontrolled, easily stirred up." It even included "being distasteful, disagreeable and bad." Based on knowing this man over several years, it was my assumption that I was not being complimented at all. I felt that I'd gotten zinged by a man wanting his way regardless of my boundary.

A word that appeared near the end of Webster's definition of "fierce" was "ardent." Now I just had to look up this new word:

"Ardent: 1. A warm or intense in feeling, passionate (ardent love). 2. Intensely enthusiastic or devoted, zealous (an ardent disciple)."

When I put the meaning of ardent with that of loyalty, I get a person who is passionate and enthusiastically devoted to faithful adherence to a person, cause, or duty. That is a cool and precise definition we should all strive to accomplish. People who have firm boundaries may appear wild, uncontrolled, and even disagreeable to those outside of recovery, or to people who do not have boundaries.

A similar story happened to a newcomer to Alcoholics Anonymous. As this man walked past the bar after a game of golf, his "friends" enticed him to come and have a few. As he declined, the jeers blamed him for the place possibly going broke if he didn't start drinking again. Ardently loyal to his recovery program, he turned and left the premises.

Develop ardent loyalty to your recovery program and the great adventure it brings to life.

If you do, then you can carry that same loyalty to your marriage and your family.

QUESTIONS

1. What kind of courage do we need for the recovery journey?

2. Where does the courage to stand against our own will come from?

3. How do we get this power into our life and use it?

4. How do we know that God is looking for ways to help us?

Fearlessly Examine Yourself

1. Precisely stated, what is it you are powerless to stop?

2. What are your character defects that you are aware of?

3. Identify some patterns of behavior concerning your character flaws and your addictive behavior.

4. What are some ways we can use to add to our list?

5. Where or with whom should we share our list?

Rebuild Your Belief System

1. What do you want to accomplish in your recovery journey?

2. Explain a stronghold.

3. What has God given to us that can destroy strongholds?

4. What is our renovation tool?

5. How do you take up the sword?

6. Find some scriptural counterparts for your character defects and write them down, e.g., unhealthy vs. healthy.

7. What can you do at the first thought of acting out a character defect? Your addictive behavior?

My Counseling Experience

1. Why would it be a good idea for you to see a skilled counselor who specializes in your addiction?

2. What are some things that have to change about you for you to have healthy relationships?

Trust God

1. What is the helmet of salvation and how do you put it on?

2. What is the effect on us when we wear the helmet?

3. Explain the meaning of trusting God.

4. When our trust in God is tested, what can we do?

5. How will God help you when your trust is tested?

Trust People

1. What are two ways that God brings healing to your life?

2. Do you have a God-sent person in your life? Explain why you think they are.

3. Are there people in your life who pull you backward? Why do you believe they do?

4. Will you talk to a skilled Christian counselor about your options?

5. List the characteristics of unhealthy intimacy.

6. List the characteristics of healthy intimacy.

7. In comparing your lists, what characteristics are manifest in your life?

8. Where can you improve and how will you start?

Setting Boundaries

1. In your own words, what is a visual illustration of a boundary?

2. What was King Solomon's advice on boundaries?

3. What was Joshua's advice on boundaries?

4. Why should we take their advice and have boundaries?

Protecting Yourself with a Red Shield

1. What is the shield of faith? Describe its power.

2. How can you use this power in setting and enforcing boundaries? List several examples.

Ardent Loyalty

1. How can ardent loyalty be of benefit to you?

CHAPTER 4
PURSUE

Philippians 3:10–15 helps me realize that no magic wand, prayer, or pill makes recovery easy:

> I want to know Christ and the power of his resurrection and the fellowship of sharing in his sufferings, becoming like him in his death, and so somehow to attain to the resurrection of the dead. Not that I have already attained all this or have already been made perfect, but I press on to take hold of that for which Christ Jesus took hold of me. Brothers, I do not consider myself yet to have taken hold of it. But one thing I do: Forgetting what is behind and straining for what is ahead, I press on toward the goal to win the prize for which God has called me heavenward in Christ Jesus. All of us who are mature should take such a view of things.

Early in my journey, this passage was a central, guiding focus. I still contemplate its meaning nearly each day. Now, let's take a walk-through these verses.

I truly wanted "to know Christ," this Jesus who came to earth so that all my wrongdoings could be forgiven. I wanted to know the Father God, who would give up his only son so I could be free from my addiction and the judgment for it, and so I could live forever in relationship with God.

I really wanted to know "the power of his resurrection." Could this power raise even me from the grave of addiction I was in? I really wanted that. Now, I know that power could and it has, but what is the depth and breadth of this power? What is the extent of this power? I wanted to know. I certainly don't know it fully yet.

I wasn't so sure about "the fellowship of sharing in his sufferings and becoming like him in his death." I didn't like suffering. I still don't. I was pretty self-centered, and being like Jesus in his death would require me to follow God's Word. Sharing in his fellowship of suffering would require me to live a life of "your will, not mine, be done." That meant doing so in the good and easy times, but especially doing so in the hard and difficult times—when I most didn't want to. But Jesus once sweat blood in the process of struggling with his will. In the end, he gave up his life for us in demonstration of the perfect mastery of the decision to turn one's will and life over to God.

The Apostle Paul wrote these verses near the end of his life. This is a significant realization when we consider that he was and remains a prime example of a Christ-follower. He wrote most of the New Testament and was profound in the depth of his wisdom. He was highly used by God. To see him write, "Not that I have already attained all this or have already been made perfect," gives me hope and helps me realize that there is so much to learn about the love of God and Jesus, our higher power. A lifetime is too brief to attain anything like the perfection Jesus had. If we could attain perfection before death, we wouldn't need a Savior. I learned in this passage that it's okay to be imperfect, it's okay to not know everything, and it's okay to need the Savior. We all do.

"Press on" is a hunting phrase meaning to pursue or run after. This is a great word to add alongside the concept of ardent loyalty in our great adventure. Paul encourages you to run after something and pursue it as though your life depended upon catching it. If you don't, you'll go hungry and eventually starve. Paul runs after understanding the whole concept of why Jesus had taken hold of him.

I wonder this myself, and I am learning that I must "press on" into God's love, commitment, care, and compassion for me, and I must pursue God's Word in every aspect of my life. This chase of faith means never doubting—not even for a millisecond—that God is faithful, trustworthy, and will keep all of his promises. Yet, even though I fall short and do not understand or have not attained all of these things, Jesus loves us with all of God's perfection, no matter where we are in the process. His only desire is that we will take his hand and allow him to guide us into knowing him more through our recovery and repentance journeys.

The more I contemplate this passage, the more I feel like Paul: I still don't understand its depth. In Paul's lifetime he still came short of fully knowing this immense higher power, Jesus Christ. He is too big to be known completely. This is why we can trust him. He is bigger than our limited intellects and therefore bigger than our problems or dilemmas. It is in a higher power like this that we can find hope and healing.

So, "forget what is behind." All of your fretting about the past will avail you nothing. Let it go. Like us, Paul had a past. His included the persecution, and even murder, of innocent people. Yet Paul reconciled with God and left these words to help us.

Leave what's behind you. "Strain for what is ahead." Put all your effort into your future. Reconcile with God and focus on your great adventure recovery program. Strive to reach the promised land here on earth and our eventual, eternal heavenly home. Put effort into helping others on the journey. Look only into the past to understand your core belief system, and only enough to remember how far God has brought you from your bondage story.

If you are maturing in your faith and in your recovery, you will "take such a view of things." My prayer is that you *will* take such a view of things. Practice, practice, practice. Stop the habitual sin in your lifetime. Pursue knowing this Jesus who loves you just the way you are, no matter where you're at in the process, but doesn't want to leave you that way. He gave his life to set you free. He rose from the dead and lives to help you understand the depth and breadth of that freedom—not just in eternity but now, *today*.

Remember, if one thing changes, many things change, and not just for you, but for those around you. Your change will bring change to your friends, your children, and your family. God will be very accepting of your healthy changes, and many people will embrace your change. Still, some won't. Regardless, pursue God and never stop pressing into him.

Difficult times will come for you that seem downright impossible. In these times, prayer is as essential as always. The armor of God passage in Ephesians 6:18 informs us that in addition to armor, we need to pray: "And pray in the Spirit on all occasions with all kinds of prayers and requests. With this in mind, be alert and always keep on praying for all the saints."

Speaking in tongues is not in my thoughts here, but rather the times I didn't even know how to pray, like the times I've felt so distraught, alone, helpless or hopeless, where all I could do was groan and maybe mutter, "God help me." Have you ever been there? It is there, on your face, with your selfish will crushed, that the Holy Spirit meets you. With your will removed, the Holy Spirit helps you and "intercedes for us with groans that words cannot express."[20] He intercedes right with the Father God. He knows how to pray on your behalf when you don't know what to pray at all.

Prayer is not about your ability. Prayer is about God and his abilities. When the Holy Spirit prays for you, your will is absent, and the prayer is in exact accord with God's will for you. Oh, that our prayers would be less about us, about what we want or how we look, and more about God's will reflected in our lives. With the Holy Spirit involved in your prayers, they will reflect a dependence on God, a life of behavioral trust in his grace and power.

We're also told to "pray in the Spirit." I believe that means praying within the perimeters of God's will for your life, i.e., the parts of his will that you know to be true for you, with all kinds of prayers and requests. God invites you into an intimate relationship with him. He wants you to talk to him a lot, in many ways, about many and all things, as it pertains to his will in your life. He wants the best for you. His promises in his Word are his will for you. He wants you to know and be assured that he will "hear [y]our prayer" and "know that we have what we asked of him" . . . "if we ask according to his will."[21]

Lastly, the Ephesians passage also tells us to "stay alert" regarding the things that would get us off track. For that reason, you must continue to do a fearless personal inventory and practice your new recovery lifestyle.

In the Apostle Peter's first letter, he informs us that the evil one is just looking for ways to destroy us. Peter also informs us to be alert, to be humble and self-controlled, to trust God, and to stand firm in our faith.[22] I believe we need to stay alert and humbly use the shield of faith as we pray for God's will to be lived out in our lives. We ought to extend our prayers to others like us. As the Ephesians text continues, it calls these people saints. My grandmother Nora had it right when she explained that the word "saints" does not refer to perfect people in some cathedral, but rather to patients within a hospital for sinners.

Such a hospital is a recovery or church group where people realize their continual need for a Savior and have accepted God through Christ as their higher power. These people have turned their wills and lives over to Christ and are presently working at transforming their belief systems to reflect God's will in their lives. These are saints, for they realize that without Jesus and the power of God in their lives they would have no hope. Pray for these people, hold them up, and pray for God's will for both your life and theirs.

In addition to wanting to know Christ, pursuing a relationship with him, and staying alert as we pray, we also need to take a stand.

Stand

I firmly believe that while you work at recovery and repentance with all the effort you can muster, you must not forget that God is at work in you through his Holy Spirit as well. You provide the willing effort while he performs the miracles. He will do for you what you cannot do for yourself. He will fulfill all of his promises.

By working at recovery and transformation, I'm not referring to working for your salvation, which is a free gift that cannot be earned. I am referring specifically to the behavioral about-face that repentance requires. God in his mercy gave you his Word to help you in your repentance journey.

Throughout the journey I've been leading you on, I have referred to the spiritual armor we need to wear as protection. Part of your work is to put on this armor. The context of this immensely powerful word of God is found in the Apostle Paul's letter to the Ephesian church. There, you will find the strength and power to *not* be swayed.

Paul tells the church (and us) to "be strong in the Lord and in his mighty power" by putting on the full armor of God. This is how you can live out the life God is calling you to live. When the desire to deviate or "fall off the wagon" comes, you will be unmoved. Just look at how unmovable Paul describes a believer who's donned the full armor of God:

> Put on the full armor of God, so that you will be able to *stand firm against* the schemes of the devil. For our struggle is not against flesh and blood, but against the rulers, against the powers, against the world forces of this darkness, against the spiritual forces of wickedness in the heavenly places. Therefore, take up the full armor of God, so that *you will be able to resist in the evil day*, and having done everything, to *stand firm. Stand firm* therefore, having girded your loins with truth, and having put on the breastplate of righteousness. (Ephesians 6:11–14)

"Stand" or "resist" appears multiple times within just a few verses. This is important and should get our attention, so let's take a deeper look at the word as it appears in each verse.

In verse 11 Paul writes that we ought to take a stand against the devil's schemes. Here, "stand" means steadfast, to be firm, to be permanent, or to endure. This "stand" refers to a single action, but for an undefined time period. The word carries with it the meaning, "each time." We are to stand each time in response to the devil's schemes. "Schemes" carries the meaning of cunning, craftiness, wiles, or sly tricks, and deceitfulness. When placed together, I follow the words "so that" in verse 11 with this: each and every time the devil presents some crafty or deceitful way to lead you off track, be firm, be permanent, and endure.

Paul tells us to put on the armor again in verse 13, followed by the use of "stand" two more times. But another word occurs before them that's also very important. A word referring to power appears in the original Greek and was translated, "You may be able" in the NIV translation. If we understand that power is behind the meaning of "You may be able," we will have a better understanding of the text.

The same Greek word for power used in this verse is the same Greek word used in Ephesians 1:21. If in fact the power of Ephesians 1:21 comes available to us by putting on the armor of God, it is a power that would be the power of God and Jesus. Their power is greater than the evil one or anything that could get us off of the track of recovery and repentance. When you use this knowledge along with your step work, you can begin to understand how "a power greater than myself can restore me." You will know that the very power of God can help you *be able to powerfully stand firm* in the face of any temptation.

All of the words for "stand" in this context carry the idea of "each time." In verse 13, "stand" is defined as "to set yourself in opposition." Clearly, if we put on the armor of God and the day of evil comes, you will have power to set yourself in opposition to it each time. The third use of the word stand has the same definition as the first: to be steadfast or firm, to be permanent and endure.

The fourth use of the word in verse 14 is defined the same, but the idea behind it is different. The first three uses of "stand" are instructional and inform us how to respond *each time* to anything or anyone who would attempt to draw us off track. Now, in the beginning of verse 14, "stand" becomes a command.

Envision a battle scene. I visualize the coliseum in the movie *Gladiator*. After training his gladiator associates to fight together, Maximus is faced for the first time with chariots descending upon him and his small band of gladiator slaves. To cut and run would certainly be a normal response in such a terrifying situation. Yet, because of their training, they knew they needed to stand firm. Because of their armor, they may have even believed they could withstand the onslaught.

In this most terrifying assault, they hear Maximus's one command: STAND!

This is the concept intended for us to understand in the Ephesian text. Like a military recruit in the midst of intense engagement with the enemy, we are to hear the command from our leader, Jesus, to stand firm in the armor of God.

Stand and use the defenses God has given you, and then you will be strong in the Lord and in his mighty power. Like Maximus with his followers, God is literally with you in your battles. In your most difficult and challenging times, God is with you, crying out the command: STAND!

Now, consider this literal translation of Ephesians 6:11–14 and how important it is that we don *every* piece of spiritual armor :

> Put on the full armor of God so that you can be firm and endure against the crafty and deceitful ways of the devil. For our struggle is not against flesh and blood, but against the rulers, against the authorities, against the powers of this dark world, and against the forces of evil in the heavenly realms. Therefore, put on the full armor of God, so that whenever the day of evil comes you may be able to have the power to set yourself in opposition to it, and after you have done everything, to be firm and endure. You are commanded to stand firm and endure, with:
>
> The belt of truth: the truth about yourself, your powerlessness over sin, and your need of a Savior.
>
> The breastplate of righteousness: you have been declared guiltless by God through the blood of Jesus. You are covered, reconciled, and returned to favor in God's eyes.
>
> The shield of faith: the Word of God is our firm conviction. We hold it up in all circumstances, base our life on it, and hide behind it. With it we close the door on all of the power of the evil one.
>
> The helmet of salvation: embrace the gospel. Believe and accept for yourself the good news that Jesus Christ died for the sins of the world and rose from the dead to set mankind free from the penalties of sin and death.
>
> The sword of the Spirit: the power to transform, renew, or rebuild our belief system comes through memorizing and contemplating God's Word in the places our beliefs need remodeling. Like a surgeon

with a scalpel, we cut out our diseased parts and engraft God's Word to bring renewal and healing.

Feet fit with the gospel of peace: a peace that passes all understanding, as described in the concluding chapter on nice shoes.

Pray in the Spirit: talk to God a lot about his will being lived out in your behavior.

Keep this in mind: stay alert. Keep doing personal inventory.

Pray for others as you do for yourself.

You are in a great spiritual battle you cannot win on your own. You have an enemy who, many times, you cannot even see. Throughout history, God has stated that he would fight his people's battles if they would stand with and trust him. God has not changed. He permanently offers his power to all of his followers.

His people fall today for the same reason they fell throughout history. They walk away from God's protective power. They cut and run when the battle starts. Putting on the armor of God is not about trying harder. It's about standing with God and trusting him and the armor he has given you. If you stand in the protection God has given you, then each time temptation comes you will "be strong in the Lord and in his mighty power." The power that created the universe, raised Jesus from the dead, calmed a sea, and directed the wind will be at your side shouting, "Stand firm! I will not leave you! I will battle with you and for you!"

You can do this! All Christ-followers fight this spiritual battle. It is important to have other people who know they are in the battle around you. We can all encourage each other to stand firm and help each other stay alert. Don't give up on the habit of meeting together in recovery or other small groups that build you up. Keep these things in mind. God wants the best for you. He demonstrated that when he gave his only son to pay the price for your sin.

The evil one wants to destroy you. Stay alert. No one cares more about you than God.

Trust his power.
Trust his armor.
Trust your new boundaries.
Pursue your renovation program.
Continually use the shield of faith.
Press on.
Stand firm.
STAND!

QUESTIONS

1. Describe the meaning of "pressing on" for your recovery.

2. How does it help you to understand that even great people like the Apostle Paul had not attained perfection?

3. What does it mean to you that Jesus Christ reached out to take hold of you?

4. What does it mean to pray in the spirit?

5. List some things you know to be God's will for your life.

6. What does God promise if you pray for his will in your life?

7. Describe how you can stay alert.

Stand

1. What does repentance require?

2. Using the definitions for "stand," write a statement applying them to your addiction or character defects. For example: "Each time I feel like viewing porn, I will not do it. I cannot serve two masters. I will set myself in opposition to viewing porn."

3. When temptation is at its greatest, who is at your side?

4. When God cries out to you to "stand," what does he tell you to do? What will he do?

5. Take your answers to question #2 and read through the meanings of each of the pieces of the armor of God. As you apply the meanings to yourself, describe what happens to your temptations.

6. Describe how you can stay alert in your recovery and repentance journey.

7. Explain for yourself what it means to be strong in the Lord and in his mighty power.

PART 5
THE PROMISED LAND

As I look back over the last twenty-four years, I can say with certainty that God keeps his promises. He has gone ahead of me, been with me, and has never left me at any point in my recovery journey.

I kept a journal through most of the first sixteen years of my recovery. This journal has helped me be accurate with my character defects, dates, and other events. Opening wide the door to my history carried some bad memories with it. I do not like who I was, but the journal reveals how far God has brought me away from my addiction to pornography and the imprint of my childhood origin experiences.

Being here in the promised land, the place we experience living in God's promises, does not mean graduation or retirement. I continue to work my recovery program as I've defined in this book. It is and how I live my life. Through God's grace and power, I will remain faithful in my trust of him.

In the final part of this journey, I'll revisit some of the promises I previously looked forward to, and I'll describe my newfound freedom, grace, and my nice shoes.

Promises Fulfilled

One of the most amazing changes that has occurred within me is my current view of pornography. I believe God has opened my eyes to see some of what he sees.

Everything about pornography is a lie. No relationship exists in pornography, and where there is no relationship, there is emptiness. This emptiness then longs to be filled with addiction, the repetitive rehearsal of behaviors lived out in the quest for meaning, purpose, happiness, and fulfillment from sources that only produce emptiness and despair.

In my mind, every porn actor is as I was. They're an addict caught in the bondage cycle of addiction. For me, to envision a porn star is parallel to envisioning the habitual drinker passed out from drinking, laying in a street gutter, covered in and sleeping in their vomit. Both images are disgusting and heartbreaking. I was crushed by the realization that I was no different than my image of them. I yearn and pray that they might find the freedom and fulfillment only God can provide.

God has truly come to live in my life. He has redeemed me. He protects me and provides for my needs. I no longer wonder if he will do these things. I have experienced it and know that he keeps his promises, and not one has failed. God has brought love and compassion to me. Abandonment is no longer a fear for me. I no longer go into hiding because I know the end of a matter will be better than how it starts out.

With no doubt in me, God has satisfied my desires with good things. He has renewed my life. I review the promises of 2 Peter 1:3–11 and know that God has called out to us because of his own glory and goodness. When we respond to his call and get to know him through his Word, his divine power gives us everything we need for life and godliness. These are realities in my life now because God has kept his promises.

God has given you very great and precious promises in his Word. When you accept those promises and trust them by applying them to your life, you can and do participate in the divine nature. You do not *become* divine, but you will experience some of what it is like. You will escape the corruption of the world caused by evil desires. I'm not kidding. We really do.

This is why it is so important to keep on adding goodness, knowledge, self-control, perseverance, godliness, brotherly kindness, and love to your firm conviction—a kind of extension of Step 12 in Alcoholics Anonymous. Doing these things keeps you effective and productive. It helps you to have clear thinking, insight, and foresight about yourself and the power of God at work in you. If you do these things, you will never fall.

I live this way now, by God's grace and through his divine power that is at work within me. It is part of God's Promised Land here on earth that we participate in his divine nature and escape the corruption of the world. In a country and a world that's out of control, this is a nice place to be. You will be here too. Trust God and his promises and follow him.

Many of my thoughts and beliefs are different now. I am a different and better person than who I was in my past. I really feel better about myself. I still have flaws. There is no perfection here. But I am in agreement with the common recovery slogan, "Progress, not perfection." I live in the contentment of Paul's statement, "Not that I have attained all this or have already been made perfect, but I press on" (Philippians 3:12). The life of recovery and repentance is not a race to see how fast you can get to a finish line or graduation ceremony. It is a process that leads to a way of life.

Without shame, I offer this image of how my recovery journey could be illustrated: I am a turtle pulling a covered wagon. No doubt the image depicts slow progress. But, by going slow I can enjoy some of the new views along the way. Plus, slow and steady progress will help me reach my destination without rolling over and crashing in the tight corners.

Living Free

The best part of being here in the Promised Land of my life is living without secrets or shame. Twenty-eight years of secrets and shame is a long time.

In the beginning I had no idea how I would ever be free of behavior that I couldn't even control. To be free of my addiction was an illusion at best. Free from my addiction to pornography and free from all the secrets is a wonderful place to be. I really like it a lot. I know you will too.

Now that I'm free, I have the wonderful opportunity to tell others. I can call out to you, "Come out! Be free!" and I'm not just an actor on a stage. God has reconciled me to himself, and he so wants to do that for you too. He loves you and deeply desires to set you free, and he won't hold anything against you that you've done. It doesn't matter if your sins are small or grossly unimaginable. There are no sins that Jesus's death and resurrection do not cover. I implore you, on Christ's behalf, "Come out! Be free! Be reconciled to God and begin the great adventure to God's promises for you. Move from secrets to freedom."

God has so expanded my territory. I have many new relationships and friends. I am involved in meaningful services to my church and the community. The new image I have gained is based on honesty and integrity rather than the ability to cover my secrets. I can't even describe how freeing that is.

This new identity in relationships is being able to *live in the present*, and not in past failures, mistakes, or arguments. I don't live in the past, but neither do I live in the future. Today I live in the here and now, this day, this moment, and I experience, participate in, and enjoy the present. I like this and so will you.

My wife, Terry, was one of the phone conversation ladies I wrote about earlier. That's right. I said I would tell you about her.

My divorce was not quite final when my father passed away. I was separated from my wife at the time. I'd been living on the road, between my children's, brothers', and parents' homes. The empathy, compassion, and care I heard in Terry's voice over the phone expressing her regret and sympathy for the loss of my father caused a gnawing desire within me to know more about this woman who actually seemed to care about me.

I didn't wait until the nearing divorce day to begin dating Terry. Both of us had been married for thirty-three years to someone else. Both of us had been in very toxic marriages that had come to an end. In each other we were finding fresh air and the hope of a second chance. Our courtship continued over the next three years. We went to professional counseling to make sure we were on the right track and not getting ourselves back into the same place we had come from. To each other, neither of us was very much like our past spouses. Most of that realization was awesome, but some differences would take getting used to.

Although we felt like two youngsters set loose in a candy store, the reality was that we were both over fifty years old and had some of those "I've always done it this way" issues. We were unorthodox in the middle of our courtship and lived together for a short time. We followed the advice of trusted friends and went back to separate housing about sixty miles apart. We continued our courtship until we married a year later. As of the writing of this book, we've been on our honeymoon for nearly nine years.

In Texas, the statement "I'll tell you what" is said to be a complete sentence, but I need to tell you what I need to tell you.

I'll tell you what: marriage without pornography is nothing short of awesome!

God has given us a second chance by reconciling us both to himself and by giving us a second chance at a healthy marriage. We are very protective of both and have boundaries to help ensure their positive growth.

I tell the story of my remarriage because only the freedom from my addiction made it possible. *You cannot be a porn or sex addict and have a healthy marriage.* Two people free from addiction and working at developing deep intimacy make for a healthier marriage.

Terry and I look for ways to live life together. We have no secrets. We are fully known to each other and have an ever-deepening intimacy. Among the things we do as small organic farmers is produce maple syrup and forage for wild crops to sell to natural food and organic restaurants. It is not uncommon for us to spend every day of March through the end of June outdoors working in and harvesting from God's garden in the wild forests of northern Wisconsin. Many days our lunch will be spread out on a large rock as our table. Our chairs are rocks, the living room is the forest around us, and the dining room is the small shore of a bubbling brook. Our music is the ever-changing sounds of water running over rocks and fallen limb. Then the kingfisher, catbird, red-breasted grosbeak and ever-present, inquisitive warblers (who relentlessly seek to impress) begins their songs. We have guests sometimes too, like deer, squirrels, wolves, bears, geese, or ducks. Once we even had a very close encounter with a very friendly beaver.

Freedom from addiction brings the opportunity to concentrate on living and enjoying life to its fullest. Everyone will not develop a profession like Terry and I. But, when your life is renovated by God through your trust in him, you will find contentment, joy, and satisfaction in numerous professions as you trust God and stop striving so hard for what is fleeting.

In the Promised Land, the never-ending quest for more material things takes a downturn as you take up the quest to live, love, and experience the simple things of life and the world that is all around you, waiting to be discovered, savored, and enjoyed.

Grace

The book of Revelation is wrapped in grace. Revelation 1:4 says, "Grace and peace to you from him who is, and who was and who is to come." The same letter ends with, "The grace of the Lord Jesus be with God's people" (Revelation 22:21).

Grace is a free and generous gift. Grace is a matter of approval and acceptance manifested by God toward man. It was common among first-century Christ-followers to greet one another and depart from each other using the salutation, "Grace and peace to you." Understanding how much they had been forgiven by God's grace made them want to extend that same grace to everyone in the known world. As you understand the shock waves of your addiction, the knowledge of just how much you have been forgiven increases. With this knowledge comes the process of making amends to people you may have harmed and extending the grace you have been given.

A Sex Addicts Anonymous slogan is, "From shame to grace." The realization of this slogan in my life is wonderful. I don't want to take one moment of it for granted. I use Lamentations 3:19–20, a passage from the great Old Testament prophet Jeremiah, to keep me on track. The following is my paraphrase:

> I remember my addiction, my wondering about with no boundaries, the abundance of shame and remorse, the endless cycle. I well remember. I know sadness and depression will follow dwelling on my past in detail for too long. Yet, if I call this fact to my mind it brings me hope. Because of God's great love for me, for you, we are not destroyed, for his compassions never fail, they are new every morning; great is your faithfulness, oh Lord, my God. The Lord God is my higher power, he has done and continues to do for me what I cannot do for myself. He is good to everyone who hopes in him and to everyone who seeks him. It is good to trust in him and wait quietly as he brings sanity and restoration to our life.

The love and power of our awesome God has brought me to this place of grace, to a place absent of shame. I like it here and so will you.

This is a time when you can work on extending grace to others. Do this for yourself and not for those you may have harmed. The people you have harmed through your addiction deserve to hear true regret for your inappropriate or hurtful behavior. If the people you have harmed choose to be gracious to you, that is a good thing. But if they choose otherwise, that is their choice and becomes an issue between them and God. It is only important that you develop graciousness toward them.

You also likely have people who have harmed you. You need to be gracious toward them and forgive them to the extent that you can. You don't need to become their friend or continue relationships with people who have been abusive to you. You can let go of your anger and resentment for others through understanding just how much you have been forgiven. Then you can forgive them and be gracious from afar.

Through the understanding of how much God has forgiven me, I can forgive the man who sexually abused me. I don't want to call him up, and I certainly won't find ways to be around him. I have prayed for him, asking God to somehow intervene in his life and bring freedom to the pain and bondage that surely must be a part of his existence. His life is in God's hands, not mine. In this case, I extend grace from a distance because it is best for me to do so. Then, forgetting what is behind I look to what is ahead.

I consider myself fortunate to have rekindled relationships with my mother and father before they passed from this life. My mother always introduced me to other people as her baby. As the youngest of three boys, I never cared for the title. As I matured in recovery, I saw her fondness and love for me in that word.

The ages of forty-eight to fifty were tough years for me. As the inevitability of divorce grew stronger and as I continued to lose hope in my marriage surviving, I spent more and more time with my son and my daughter. I also visited my brothers' homes fairly often. I literally lived between all of their homes for quite some time.

During this time, my son taught me how to ride horses. This was quite a task since his middle-aged father was scared to death of those critters. I would rather meet up with a wolf or a bear in the wilderness with no gun—and that's happened to me—than get on the back of one of my biggest fears.

At the same time, my daughter was inspiring me to run—also a task I dreaded. I had never run more than the length of a football field except when the coaches assigned me to the

800-meter relay team in track and field. The farthest I'd ever run before then was one hundred yards. Why run now, at my age, when walking and driving a car seemed so much more practical (if not civilized)?

My son worked mercifully to teach me to ride horses while my daughter's marathon coach, who had trained her as a fundraising runner for a Leukemia/Lymphoma organization, trained me for their marathon fundraising team. A year of effort went into my trainings. Around the time I was turning fifty years old, I suffered the death of my thirty-two-year-old marriage. Within several months of each other, I placed in a thirty-mile endurance race riding a high-spirited, prancing Arabian horse, and I ran a 26.2-mile marathon averaging ten minutes per mile. The races were certainly accomplishments, but more importantly my children had taught me healthy ways of coping with hardship in life.

They had extended grace to me.

I remember calling my mom around this time. She was in an assisted living facility quite some distance away.

"Hi mom, it's your baby ... Lynn."

She was silent, but then came the words I'll never forget: "Oh, I don't call him my baby any more. He has proven himself to be a man."

She gave me the most gracious gift a parent can give their child. I cried.

My mom and dad had been married for over sixty-seven years. No one in my immediate family, and only several in my whole family history of three generations in America and back into German roots, had ever gone through a divorce. My parents could have been critical of me, yet they built me up, supported me, and blessed me.

After my remarriage, my mom wanted Terry and I to visit her as she had something she wanted to give us. During that visit, my mother had us kneel in front of her. She laid her hands on our heads and blessed our marriage—a gift money cannot buy, a gift called grace.

My oldest brother has always been an inspiration to me. He is full of grace and extends it freely. My relationship with my other brother is a work-in-progress. I follow the example that has been demonstrated to me and I extend grace to him. The three of us and our wives get together several times a year, and it is always a good experience. Grace and a little humor bring us closer in relationship.

I state again that I have been forgiven much, and I have earned no privilege to withhold grace and forgiveness from others. I believe being angry, resentful, or vengeful would only cause harm to me and the people around me. I also think of the people who don't want to forgive me.

As of this writing, my son who was so gracious to me has not talked to me in over five years. I can understand some reasons. Being angry over issues while growing up is certainly a part of his anger. And why wouldn't that be so? Addictive households are dysfunctional and leave imprints. I am part of that past. I can't make anyone forgive me. I can only ask for forgiveness for the ways I have hurt him or fallen short of his expectations. Then all I can do is extend grace to him and others who fall into this misfortunate impasse. I pray nearly every day that the wall might come down for us to talk and be a part of each other's lives again. My son is married and has two children.

My daughter is very gracious and our relationship is growing ever deeper. She continues to inspire me. She is a very accomplished writer, and we are very proud of how she has worked through her childhood of origin issues to emerge as a great help to others who struggle. She's married to a wonderful man whom we are proud of, and they have three boys we adore.

I have another daughter who has lived a life of addiction and is currently nearing one year of sobriety. Time will tell if she will stay in recovery this time. However, I am excited that this is her longest sobriety in seventeen years. She's making good choices and behaving responsibly in her personal life and in caring for her three children. I wait in a graciousness that has boundaries.

I have gained a wonderful and gracious daughter through my remarriage, a great son-in-law, and two grandsons. I am blessed.

God's Promised Land on earth *isn't* perfect. It is flawed, but it is the best place on earth. Even though there are still struggles, instead of acting out in an addiction that brought despair and destruction to me and most all my relationships, now there is reward. Most all of my relationships are growing stronger and deeper in intimacy than I have ever experienced before. I have never been happier. And I know that God is able to do things I cannot. He has a long history of reaching people through one of his most outstanding character traits: grace.

Nice Shoes

The final piece of the armor of God we're encouraged to don are shoes, but not just any shoes. "Have your feet fitted with the readiness that comes from the gospel of peace" (Ephesians 6:15) The gospel is all about what Jesus did for you and all of mankind.

Colossians 2:13–15 helps us understand that even while you were dead in our sins—or while you were in the height of your addiction—God made you alive in Christ. He forgave all your sins. God canceled all the laws that made you guilty. He took the laws and your sin and nailed them to a cross that he hung upon. He paid the price for the sins you were guilty of. He took your place. In doing this God himself disarmed all of the evil powers. They have lost all right to criticize or condemn you. The paraphrase and the meaning of these words are amazing: God through Christ has set you free. All you need to do is accept that fact and you are free, forgiven, and eternally alive in Christ.

When you accept God's forgiveness, you can truly begin to experience the peace that God through Jesus can bring to you. Everything God is about is to see people come to this place of knowing. He and he alone can fill the emptiness that you try to fill in countless other ways. By design, the creator God of the universe left an emptiness within mankind that can only be filled through a relationship with him. He is the perfect fit, the perfect match.

When you let him fill the void within you, a peace that passes all human understanding is one result. The inner peace I have found by trusting God and accepting the gospel for myself has brought a peace to my life I have never before experienced. This is serenity. It is like finding the missing piece to the puzzle.

Now I feel complete.

Contentment is another benefit of accepting the gospel of peace. I have less money and fewer toys than I had through my addiction years, on the former shore of my Red Sea. However, I have a contentment that I never had before, and I like it a lot. Psalm 46:10 states, "Be still and know that I am God." The Hebrew word for "be still" means "to cease striving." When you drop all of your attempts at being complete by your own efforts and come to believe that the creator God can and will do for you what you cannot do for yourself, you will then experience the fulfilling contentment that comes from knowing God.

My wife and I experience times when we are not sure how we will make ends meet financially. But as we look back, we see that God has met our every need. Sometimes circumstances have been altered, as if by someone else. Even disastrous equipment breakdowns have turned out to be blessings in the end. I can't explain how this works. All I know is that it does.

In the spring of 2013, we were in the middle of a major run of maple sap, which we harvest and process into maple syrup. Sap flowed so quickly that my wife and I worked sixteen-hour days to keep up with its collection and processing. We were tired, but the seasonal harvest is a major part of our income.

It was a Saturday and I needed the following morning off to teach a class on Revelation. A large group of adults had signed up for the first session of the class that I had already devoted over 400 hours of research to. I was also the scheduled worship leader for two Sunday morning services at my church's fellowship. So why couldn't I miss just a day?

During sap runs the first ten to twelve hours of every day are devoted to processing. If I fall behind, I won't have enough storage for the new sap coming in. I saw no other way to teach the class than to let the new sap just flow over onto the ground—money draining into the earth.

Since I decided to trust him, God has always provided for me. I made teaching the class and leading worship the priority. On April 13, 2013, I wrote in my sapping journal: "Stay tuned. Two worship services and I need to teach a class tomorrow. God will show the way."

I awoke Sunday morning to an unusual and unpredicted

arctic blast of air so cold it had frozen the trees solid, including the sap in the bags, the tube lines, the transfer tanks, and the outside storage tanks. The weather had shut down all new sap collection for at least twenty-four hours. I was able to fulfill my commitment to God and my church family that morning, then use the afternoon and evening to process the sap in indoor storage. I even slept in on Monday morning.

That felt good. Even better, we didn't lose *one cent* of production. Someone might say that this event was coincidence. That's a possibility, but I don't think so. God's intervention is far more probable. I have recorded in my journals and can recall too many of these interventions to think they're mere coincidences.

I have come to believe that God is living and active in my life. He is not limited to my intellect, or to human logic, or by the laws of man or nature. God is above all these things and is looking for ways he can show himself faithful to any person who will trust him, including you. Contentment is the result of trusting God and is most manifest when we understand and become convinced that when we are at our most powerless, he is at his most powerful.

Wearing the shoes of the good news is to know and to look back at a few days, weeks, or years and realize that God is restoring your life and doing for you what you cannot do for yourself. The Lord God of Israel, the fulfilled prophecy of the Messiah, Jesus Christ, and their continuous manifestation through the living Holy Spirit and written word are the only Higher Power that is living and active to restore your life. The result of letting God redeem and restore me is a peace and contentment I refer to as "nice shoes." Like perfectly fitting running shoes makes distance running comfortable, having a relationship with the living God is the perfect fit to making your life the best it can be. My life attests to this fact.

My intention has been that the words I've written are a testimony that will draw you into a relationship with this great God who so desires a relationship with you. I pray that you will trust this very Lord and God. I pray you will decide to follow him as he leads you on the great adventure he has led me. He will never lead you by force, but he will go before you, be behind you, and be at your side if you surrender your will and your life to him and willingly follow him.

As you follow him, I pray that your character will be rebuilt into the character of the living God. May his grace surround you as you experience his many and very great promises for you. He loves you and wants his very best for you.

May you experience God's presence in your daily life. I pray that you will come to the place in this earthly life, this Promised Land of the present, that you will be free from your sin of choice and free from your addiction, and in your freedom you will breathe deeply the peace of God. I pray you'll be able to look down at your feet one day and say, "Wow! Nice shoes." I pray that, in time, others will say the same of your "shoes" as well.

God's grace will surround you on your great adventure.

You can do this.

Now is the time.

None of his promises will fail you. They will all be true.

Take that first step to cross your Red Sea and God will be with you every step thereafter.

Surrender your will to the one who died in your place.

Pick up the shield of faith, protect yourself with it, and follow God on the greatest adventure of your life, from former addict to free-from-sin Christ-follower.

QUESTIONS

Promises Fulfilled

1. What are some promises that are now true for you? Include any and all, even if they're partially true.

Living Free

1. What freedoms or other benefits are you experiencing as you extend the days, weeks, or months of sobriety from your addiction?

Grace

1. How does grace extended to you feel?

2. Are you ready to ask for grace? From whom?

3. Are you ready to extend grace? To whom?

4. What can you do when someone does not want to extend grace to you?

Nice Shoes

1. When you trust God and accept for yourself what Jesus did on the cross for you, what can happen for you? List at least nine benefits. Add to this list over time as God reveals to you all of his benefits.

THE TWELVE STEPS OF ALCOHOLICS ANONYMOUS, ADAPTED FOR ANY ADDICTION

1. We admitted we were powerless over our _____ addiction—that our lives had become unmanageable.
2. Came to believe that a power greater than ourselves could restore us to sanity.
3. Made a decision to turn our will and our lives over to the care of God as we understood Him.
4. Made a searching and fearless moral inventory of ourselves.
5. Admitted to God, to ourselves, and to another human being the exact nature of our wrongs.
6. Were entirely ready to have God remove all these defects of character.
7. Humbly asked Him to remove our shortcomings.
8. Made a list of all persons we had harmed, and became willing to make amends to them all.
9. Made direct amends to such people wherever possible, except when to do so would injure them or others.
10. Continued to take personal inventory and when we were wrong promptly admitted it.
11. Sought through prayer and meditation to improve our conscious contact with God as we understood Him, praying only for knowledge of His will for us and the power to carry that out.
12. Having had a spiritual awakening as the result of these steps, we tried to carry this message to others and to practice these principles in all our affairs.

ENDNOTES

1. a. *The Greek New Testament* (New York: American Bible Society, 2014).

b. Harold Moulton, ed., *The Analytical Greek Lexicon* (Grand Rapids, MI: Zondervan Publishing, 1978).

c. Eric G. Jay, *New Testament Greek: An Introductory Grammar* (Southampton: The Camelot Press, 1975).

d. Walter Baur, William F. Arndt, trans., and F. Wilbur Gingrich, trans., *A Greek English Lexicon of the New Testament and Other Early Christian Literature* (Chicago: University of Chicago Press, 1952).

e. *The Bible: New International Version* (Grand Rapids, MI: Zondervan Bible Publishers). Note: All Bible references are from the New International Version unless otherwise noted.

2. Patrick Carnes, *Don't Call It Love: Recovery From Sexual Addiction* (New York: Bantam Books, 1991).

3. Patrick Carnes, *Sexual Anorexia: Overcoming Sexual Self-Hatred* (Center City, MN: Hazelden Publishing, 1997).

4. Exodus 13:21-22.

5. Isaiah 52:12.

6. Luke 16:13.

7. Ephesians 5:11–14; Matthew 6:24; John 3 19–21; 1 Corinthians 10:21; Romans 13:12; Psalm 32:3–4; Psalm 38:4.

8. Ephesians 2:18–21.

9. Patrick Carnes, *The Betrayal Bond: Breaking Free of Exploitive Relationships* (Deerfield Beach, FL: Health Communications Inc., 1997).

10. Bryn C. Collins. *Emotional Unavailability: Recognizing It, Understanding It, and Avoiding Its Trap* (Contemporary Books, 1997).

11. Psalm 34:4.

12. Paul D. Meier et al., *A Walk With the Serenity Prayer: Daily Devotions for People in Recovery* (Nashville, TN: Thomas Nelson, 1991).

13. Deuteronomy 10:13–14.

14. *The Bible*: New King James Translation.

15. Francis Brown, S. R. Driver, and Charles A. Briggs. *The New Brown-Driver-Briggs-Gesenius Hebrew and English Lexicon* (Peabody, MA: Hendrickson Publishers, 1979).

16. John 2:24–25.

17. Bryn C. Collins. *Emotional Unavailability: Recognizing It, Understanding It, and Avoiding Its Trap* (Contemporary Books, 1997).

18. Patrick Carnes, *Don't Call It Love: Recovery From Sexual Addiction* (New York: Bantam Books, 1991).

19. Proverbs 4:13.

20. Romans 8:26–27.

21. 1 John 5:14–15.

22. 1 Peter 5:6–11.

CREDITS AND SOURCES OF HELP

Mark Laaser, M.Div, Ph.D

Author of *Faithful and True: Sexual Integrity in a Fallen World*

Faithful and True Clinic

www.faithfulandtrue.com

15798 Venture Ln.

Eden Prairie, MN 55344

952-746-3880

Sex Addicts Anonymous (SAA)

P.O. Box 70949

Houston, TX 77270

713-869-4902

Sex and Love Addicts Anonymous (SLAA)

P.O. Box 111910

West Newton, MA 02165-0010

Sexaholics Anonymous (SA)

www.sexaholicsanonymous.org

ABOUT THE AUTHOR

Lynn Fredrick has a B.A. in theology and psychology, 1980, from Minnesota Bible College, now known as Cross Roads Bible College, in Rochester, MN. Lynn has been married to his best friend Terry for nine years. They have a total of four adult children and ten grandchildren.

Lynn is an elder with the First Church of Christ fellowship in the northern Wisconsin community of Ladysmith. He is semi-retired to a small organic farm and enjoys living in God's earthly garden. With twenty-four years of sobriety from a twenty-eight year addiction to pornography, Lynn is a speaker and author dedicated to sharing his story in the hope to help people escape the destroying fire of pornography and other sexual addiction.

To contact him, call 715-532-9908 or leave an e-mail at his public library: ltgodspromise@gmail.com

Lynn Fredrick
W8756 W. Townline Road
Ladysmith, WI 54848
715-532-9908

www.lynnfredrick.com

www.ingramcontent.com/pod-product-compliance
Lightning Source LLC
Chambersburg PA
CBHW071710040426
42446CB00011B/1992